'As a university media and public relations instructor with a Ph.D. in communication, I am deeply immersed in the ever-evolving world of branding and greatly admire new perspectives that inform how theories apply in daily practice. It is with this lens that I wholeheartedly endorse the groundbreaking textbook 'Strategic Brand Licensing.' Co-authored by Professor M. Cristina Longo and Pete Canalichio, a renowned expert in brand licensing, this book offers a profound understanding of the symbiotic relationship between branding and licensing. It seamlessly merges cutting-edge marketing theories with practical insights from brand licensing, making it an indispensable resource for students and professionals alike. The authors' combined expertise ensures readers gain a holistic perspective on leveraging brands effectively. This textbook is a must-read, unlocking the full potential of strategic brand licensing.'

Heather Epkins, PhD, *University of Maryland, College Park*

'With an easy-to-read style of writing, Strategic Brand Licensing by Cristina Longo and Pete Canalichio is filled with fascinating insights into the history of branding, as well as what to expect throughout each process of the brand licensing journey. As someone who is expanding my business brand, I have found some incredibly useful ideas to percolate on and develop with my team as we scale my business. And you can guarantee that this book will become our bible to brand expansion and licensing!'

Dawn Bates, *bestselling author and writing coach*

'In the dynamic world of branding and marketing, brand licensing has emerged as a powerful tool for businesses to expand their reach, enhance brand equity, and generate new revenue streams. Strategic Brand Licensing: Building Brand Value Through Enduring Partnerships by Maria Cristina Longo and Pete Canalichio provides an insightful and up-to-date exploration of the brand licensing landscape, equipping students with the knowledge and skills to navigate this complex and ever-evolving field.

The book masterfully delves into the intricacies of brand licensing, covering a wide spectrum of topics, from the fundamental principles and legal aspects to the strategic considerations and practical applications. Students will gain a deep understanding of the various types of licensing agreements, the different licensing models, and the key considerations for both licensors and licensees.

What sets this textbook apart is its ability to strike a balance between theoretical rigor and practical application. Longo and Canalichio seamlessly integrate real-world examples, case studies, and industry insights throughout the text, allowing students to connect the dots between theoretical concepts and practical implementation. This approach not only enhances the learning experience but also prepares students for successful careers in brand licensing.

Moreover, the book's engaging writing style and clear organization make it an enjoyable read for students of all backgrounds. The authors clearly explain complex concepts using straightforward language and provide ample illustrations to enhance understanding.

This comprehensive textbook is an invaluable resource for students pursuing a career in brand licensing. It provides a thorough grounding in the fundamentals of the field while also offering practical guidance for navigating the complexities of licensing agreements, strategic partnerships, and global licensing opportunities

T0299759

Whether you are a student seeking a comprehensive introduction to brand licensing or an experienced professional seeking to refresh your knowledge, this textbook is an essential resource. It provides the tools and insights necessary to understand, strategize, and implement successful brand licensing initiatives.

I highly recommend this textbook for adoption in college courses on brand licensing. The book's comprehensive coverage, engaging writing style, and practical approach make it an ideal resource for students at all levels of academic expertise.

I am confident that this textbook will become a staple in the field of brand licensing education, empowering students to become the next generation of brand licensing professionals.'

Andrea Seeger-Doring, *founder and CEO, The Marketing Drill, LLC,*
Team UP to 10X, LLC, and Digitus Medius Enterprises, Inc.

'Strategic *Brand Licensing* is a groundbreaking collaboration between two luminaries in the field of branding and licensing, Professor Cristina Longo and Pete Canalichio. As a university executive, I'm impressed by their comprehensive approach to this subject. This book seamlessly bridges academic theory and practical industry insights, making it an invaluable resource for students and professionals alike. Longo's academic rigor combined with Canalichio's real-world experience offers a unique perspective on brand expansion and licensing. Their work not only enriches the academic discourse but also equips future leaders with the knowledge and skills needed to navigate this complex and ever-evolving landscape. A must-read for anyone seeking to master brand licensing.'

Kristina Clement, *Associate Dean, Georgia Institute of Technology*

'As a university professor in the field of international business, global sourcing in international entrepreneurial management at the international program of the Belgian Thomas More business school, I am thrilled to endorse the groundbreaking textbook 'Strategic Brand Licensing' coauthored by an Italian university marketing professor and an American brand licensing expert. This collaborative effort transcends geographical boundaries, offering a global perspective on the intricacies of brand licensing. The book adeptly fuses European finesse in marketing with American industry expertise, providing a comprehensive and culturally diverse understanding of this strategic discipline. The very clearly developed theoretical chapters, combined with hands-on tools and methods and completed with enlightening international case material, makes this publication a must-read for any professional aiming to navigate the complex landscape of brand licensing successfully as well as for any students in preparation for a professional career in this area at a global level.'

Alexander Deblond, *Thomas More University of Applied Sciences*

'Continue the Brand Licensing race in a fast read follow-up to Canalichio's Expand, Grow, Thrive: 5 Proven Steps to Turn Good Brands into Global Brands! The wisdom in this volume of Strategic Brand Licensing Building Brand Value Through Enduring Partnerships is a marathon of winning insights and valuable case studies which share the real world results of successful (and not-so-successful) Brand Licensing initiatives. Equally invigorating is the matter-of-fact story telling Longo and Canalichio share in guiding us on the multi-faceted strategic journey to deliver "enduring, profitable and successful" business value via wise licensing partnerships. As a seasoned Financial Executive, I immediately see the correlation between these experts' guidance and the winning business licensing decisions other executives can make to harness profitable growth in their own brand licensing experience. True to his Naval Aviator experience, Canalichio provides a valuable Check-List approach of do's and don'ts in the Licensing Deal Making process plus numerous templates for those with a Need for Speed.'

Bill Huber, *former Chief Financial Officer, VELUX Group USA, Inc.*

'It's been a privilege to read this comprehensive book about strategic brand licensing and come to fully appreciate this dynamic and exciting field. Longo and Canalichio bring a wealth of experience and provide a compelling roadmap for licensees and licensors, replete with insightful examples, success stories, and first-person interviews of founders and CEOs. It includes how-to guides, a sample term sheet and business plan template, and much more, giving participants the necessary materials to jumpstart licensing programs in any industry.

From the origins of licensing an image of Mickey Mouse by Walt Disney nearly 100 years ago, to the more recent auctioning of digital fine art through NFTs, licensing has become an over $340 billion trade spanning industries like entertainment, sports, art, and consumer products. *Strategic Brand Licensing* explains what licensing is, how it works and doesn't – as in Harley Davidson *perfume* or Evian Water *bras* – and provides key take-aways, like developing win-win strategies and to avoiding those that 'slap logos on everything.'

Specifically, the authors explain how to develop licensing programs, determine the license-ability of brands, and how to select a licensee or target a licensor with analytical processes and checklists. From tools that facilitate licensing, like brand licensing software, to discussions of common pitfalls and recommendations to avoid them, *Strategic Brand Licensing* captures the key components for making successful licensing partnerships, and it keeps the reader captivated through real-life stories of celebrities and influencers like Michael Jordan and Aarin Burch.

Numerous case studies illustrate concepts, such as how Ferrari pivoted to extend its brand into a lifestyle brand when its extension into sedans and sportscars didn't connect with consumers.

As a lifelong product management professional, Longo and Canalichio have revealed the vast opportunities of licensing and even made me wonder if I might have missed my calling as a brand manager or owner developing win-win licensing relationships. They have succeeded in showing how licensing is used as a growth strategy and how useful it will be for our own business.

Strategic Brand Licensing is a 'must-read' for those of you seeking to grow your business and your brand.'

Kevin Cochran, *CEO and founder, Jackie Mays Burger*

STRATEGIC BRAND LICENSING

This book presents a roadmap for a brand licensing strategy to enable companies to leverage brand value and expand into other product categories or into different markets. Readers will understand both the risks and the benefits of partnerships, how to make the most of a brand's potential in the digital platform and how to extend a product portfolio through established brands. Brand licensing can be of interest to many stakeholders, including large companies, entrepreneurs, retailers, agencies and even celebrities. This is also a relevant strategy for small- and medium-sized enterprises that want to expand their business abroad, reconciling their limited size with their flexibility. Examples of long-standing partnerships are presented and analyzed, with detailed consideration of what has made them so successful.

Through the presentation of case studies in the sectors particularly interested in brand licensing, including the art, character, entertainment, fashion, jewelry, sports and toys sectors, this book aims to highlight opportunities, limits and challenges from both the licensor and licensee's perspectives. In particular, these case studies represent an effective basis for comparing different experiences and brand licensing strategies, allowing readers to understand both best practices and pitfalls to avoid when building an effective and enduring licensing program. Chapter objectives, summaries, key learning points and discussion questions reinforce understanding and aid reflection.

Practical yet theoretically grounded, this book is particularly suitable for postgraduate, MBA and executive education students interested in strategic brand management, licensing strategy and brand expansion. This book can also serve as a valuable guide for professionals interested in expanding their brand portfolio.

This book provides effective tools to evaluate the strategic side of brand licensing and the selection of the appropriate company to be a licensee. Online resources include PowerPoint slides, a test bank of exam questions, a case list and discussion questions.

Maria Cristina Longo is Associate Professor of Business Economics and Management at the University of Catania, Italy. She was Canon Foundation in Europe 2021 Research Fellow.

Pete Canalichio is a top-tier consultant specializing in brand expansion and licensing, a TEDx speaker, an award-winning author and a former US Navy pilot.

STRATEGIC BRAND LICENSING

Building Brand Value through
Enduring Partnerships

Maria Cristina Longo and Pete Canalichio

Routledge
Taylor & Francis Group

LONDON AND NEW YORK

Designed cover image: axllll/Getty Images

First published 2024
by Routledge
4 Park Square, Milton Park, Abingdon, Oxon OX14 4RN

and by Routledge
605 Third Avenue, New York, NY 10158

Routledge is an imprint of the Taylor & Francis Group, an informa business

British Library Cataloguing-in-Publication Data
A catalogue record for this book is available from the British Library

ISBN: 9781032428499 (hbk)
ISBN: 9781032428482 (pbk)
ISBN: 9781003364566 (ebk)

DOI: 10.4324/9781003364566

Typeset in Galliard
by Apex CoVantage, LLC

Access the Support Material: www.routledge.com/9781032428482

CONTENTS

CONTENTS

ABOUT THE AUTHORS

Author Cristina Longo

Maria Cristina LONGO
Associate Professor of Business Economics and Management, University of Catania, Catania, Italy

Cristina Longo is Associate Professor of Business Economics and Management at the University of Catania (Italy). She holds a laurea degree with 110 summa cum laude and a PhD in Business Administration. Her research interests focus on the topics of strategy, innovation management and entrepreneurship. She was Canon Foundation in Europe 2021 Research Fellow at Yokohama National University, Japan.

Author Pete Canalichio

Pete CANALICHIO
Managing Partner, Licensing Brands, Inc. DBA BrandAlive, Atlanta, USA

Pete Canalichio is an award-winning author of the Amazon #1 New Release, "Expand, Grow, Thrive" (2018) and a TEDx speaker. He has worked in brand expansion and licensing for the past 25 years for The Coca-Cola Company, Newell Brands and, most recently, BrandAlive, a Service-Disabled Veteran Owned Small Business that he founded in 2009.

Pete attended the US Naval Academy, where he earned a BS in physics. Pete earned his MBA from the University of North Carolina Kenan-Flagler Business School, where he was a Richard H. Jenrette fellow and salutatorian of his class. Throughout his career, Pete has operated in the global arena, having worked in more than 40 countries and managed extensive projects across national and continental borders.

CASES

PREFACE – TOO BIG TO IGNORE

Maura J. Regan

Welcome to the world of brand licensing!

The beauty of this industry is that, as soon as you understand licensing, you'll realize you're surrounded by it in your everyday life. At this very moment, if you look around, you're likely to see several licensed products. In fact, you might even be wearing a licensed item.

Technically, licensing is the process of allowing a third party (licensee) to manufacture and distribute products or experiences featuring a brand, character or image under license from the owner (licensor). But more than that, licensing extends the emotional connection between a consumer and a brand – ultimately driving revenue. Lots of revenue.

Licensing International's 2023 Global Licensing Industry Study reported that sales of licensed products and merchandise reached $340.8 billion in 2022, an increase of 8 percent compared to the year before and a record for the industry. Brands across the entertainment, sports and corporate categories drove much of that growth, as did the massive increase in demand for location-based entertainment. And the market is only expected to continue to expand, with Business Research Insights recently projecting the licensing industry will reach $422.5 billion by 2031.

Licensing might be a formula you can apply to your business, but it's also an art form. Not every licensed product or experience is created equally, and in order to truly connect with consumers, it's crucial not only to understand their shifting needs but also to develop a deep understanding of the different forms of licensing that exist, the distribution and retail formats best suited to your offerings, the current trends informing strategic decisions throughout the industry, and how to create and nurture partnerships within the brand licensing community.

Those partnerships are especially important because every step of the licensing process requires collaboration. From negotiating the commercial terms of a deal to developing creative assets to ultimately approving the product, the licensor and licensee must work together in order to bring a brand to life in a new way. Each partner's expertise is needed to expand the intellectual property (IP) into a new category or reach a new demographic.

The very best of these partnerships are like marriages. They evolve over time, constantly changing as each partner gains new experiences and fresh perspectives. They are the foundation of the brand licensing deals that inform our lives and occupy pop culture – years from now academics will still be studying the "Summer of Barbie" and how Mattel and Warner Bros. Discovery formed the engine behind more than 100 licensing agreements.

But, like any partnership, licensing deals can fall apart. In my more than 20 years of experience in the global brand licensing and media industries, I've witnessed everything from bankruptcies to celebrity ambassadors making statements that were antithetical to a brand's values. In most cases, however, licensed offerings that fail to connect with consumers simply missed the mark. If the product doesn't feel true to the brand, consumers will sense it immediately.

For most of us in the global brand licensing industry, these lessons have been learned through years of hard work and built upon the experiences of those who came before us. It's a common refrain in our community that we didn't choose licensing – it found us. It's rare to find a licensor or licensee who specifically set out to be a part of this wonderful world. But that's changing.

It's crucial that the next generation of licensing professionals have opportunities to learn about the industry at all stages of their educational journey. Providing resources to these young talents is part of our mission to foster the expansion of brand licensing around the world and to advance the understanding of licensing in society.

This book, which Cristina Longo and Pete Canalichio have put so much love and effort into, is a perfect example of the kind of resources that are needed to support emerging licensing executives as they enter our industry. I am so looking forward to the textbooks that will be written years from now, spotlighting the groundbreaking licensing deals these rising stars will one day broker.

Maura J. Regan Biography

Bringing more than 20 years of global licensing and media experience, Maura Regan joined Licensing International, the leading trade organization for the brand licensing industry, in December 2016. Since 2018, she has served as President of Licensing International and is responsible for promoting the growth and expansion of licensing around the world. Former head of global consumer products at Sesame Workshop, the home of Sesame Street, Maura J. Regan held executive positions with MTV Networks, Scholastic Entertainment and The Jim Henson Company. Maura Regan is a standing fellow of the US-Japan Foundation Leadership Program and on the advisory board of One Animation, The Toy Foundation and Women in Toys. Recognized as a top leader in business by Irish-America magazine, Maura J. Regan was also a recipient of the K.I.D.S. (now Delivering Good) Women of Achievement Award. In 2019 she was named "Volunteer of the Year" by NYSAE. She earned a Bachelor of Arts degree in Art History from the University of Massachusetts at Amherst.

Maura J. Regan, President of Licensing International

INTRODUCING THE BRAND LICENSING WORLD

With a market size in 2022 of $315.5 billion globally with a growth rate of 8 percent over prior year, the brand licensing industry is projected to reach $384.5 billion by 2028 and grow to $422.6 billion by 2031 according to Business Research Insights (Brand Licensing Market Report, 2023). As such, brand licensing today has a profound influence on the competitive strategies of all companies. The goal of this book is to introduce brand owners and managers to the world of brand licensing. Brand licensing is a growth strategy that is based on the ability to leverage brand value (Gupta et al., 2020) by expanding and extending it into other product categories. Through partnerships with producers, distributors and agents, the brand-owning (Börjeson & Boström, 2018) company can focus on growth based on the valorization of intangible resources and assets. Brand licensing strategy allows licensors to have non-monetary benefits (Christensen & Nikolaev, 2013) in terms of increased brand breadth, greater brand depth, technology transfer and higher business value.

Brand licensing can be of interest to many stakeholders, including large companies, entrepreneurs, retailers, agencies and even celebrities. This is a relevant strategy also for small- and medium-sized enterprises that want to expand their business abroad, reconciling their limited size with their flexibility in achieving their desired expansion. It also involves many fields of activities, including music, art, luxury, fashion, sport, celebrity and character. Strategic brand licensing management (Chernev, 2020) requires partner selection, activities planning and performance evaluation. Essential components in the brand licensing strategy are managing the relationship between the partners involved, developing a durable and valuable program, using appropriate tools to evaluate brand licensing and executing the program according to objectives and results previously set by the partners. Brand licensing is a choice that exposes both licensors and licensees to business risk (Sadgrove, 2016), operational risks (Araz et al., 2020) but also risk of loss of brand value. Some examples of business risk are poor business results that come from poor program management, brand expansion into a weak brand/wrong category, lack of licensee capability (Somaya et al., 2011), selection of the wrong licensee, complexity of events, behavior of celebrities, theft from piracy/counterfeiting. These increases in business risk due to their

DOI: 10.4324/9781003364566-1

nature almost always result in an increase in brand risk. Understanding who the brand owner is partnering with, how much value lies in the licensed brand and how to set up and manage a licensing program are topics of strategic importance when considering brand growth through licensing (Sherman, 2011). Likewise, running a licensing program, taking on the risk of commercializing products with licensed brands (Cardinali et al., 2019) and expanding into product categories other than the original ones are relevant aspects for those who decide to become a licensee (Canalichio, 2019). This book, therefore, considers brand licensing from the dual perspective of licensors and licensees. It is intended to be a valuable guide for brand owners, entrepreneurs and managers in their decision to expand their brand portfolio across channels, markets or regions, or to extend their product portfolio into new categories through the licensing way (Kirca et al., 2020). At the same time, it intends to actively support licensed companies, especially small ones, which make use of this tool to grow externally with fewer capital constraints.

The core message of this book is that brand licensing is like a marathon with great expectations, but also with numerous failures, where learning practices and pitfalls to avoid these are of strategic importance for building an effective and enduring licensing program. Texts and manuals on this topic are limited in number and often address brand licensing from a technical point of view (Goldscheider & Gordon, 2006; Parr, 2007; Raugust, 2004; Steenkamp, 2017). Particularly, some studies (Desai, 2012; Gibson, 2006; Sáiz & Castro, 2018) are focused on the legal side of licensing and others (Joshi & Yadav, 2019; Heath et al., 2011; Pina et al., 2010; Salinas & Pérez, 2009) on brand expansion and extension from a brand perspective, but the gap on brand expansion and extension in terms of licensing strategy is underexplored.

This book emphasizes the strategic side of licensing as a core way to implement branding strategy, and extract value through shared risk, business and market. The volume considers the perspective of the licensor and the licensees in determining whether licensing is the most effective option to meet their business goals and growth objectives. It also looks at how licensors and licensees work together in the licensing program and the impact of this collaboration to discover areas of overlapping improvements and effectiveness.

The text provides analytical tools to evaluate the effectiveness of the program, to enhance a company's flagship brand or to enter different markets or businesses. Readers will learn how to build the brand licensing program step-by-step, to realize the brand's potential or to extend the product portfolio through established brands. Each chapter includes case studies of enduring partnerships and pop-ups dedicated to specific examples of brand licensing. The presentation of case studies in sectors particularly interested in brand licensing, including Sports, Character, Communication, Entertainment, Fashion, Toys, Gardens, Education and Music, aims to highlight the situation in which the agreement occurs, opportunities, limits and challenges for the licensor and licensees. In particular, the case studies allow readers to compare different experiences relating to actors, countries, sectors and options in order to understand decisions, criteria and results concerning business growth according to brand licensing. We selected case studies according to the direction of the growth, expansion versus extension, core business versus services (complementarity), expansion in the same geographical area versus expansion in other geographical areas, increasing in value versus decreasing in value, over the short, medium and long term.

The STAR Method is used throughout the book for illustrating case studies that reinforce the subjects presented. STAR stands for *Situation*, *Task*, *Action* and *Result*, and it's designed to help structure and illustrate the examples in a clear and concise way. Where warranted, *Noteworthy* comments are provided that emphasize context, results or other interesting aspects of the case that arise. Below is a breakdown of each component. *Situation*: This section sets the stage for what was going on and provides context for the case. *Task*: An explanation of the specific task or goal needed to solve the problem to be solved is presented. This clarifies what the participants are trying to achieve. *Action*: The section details the actions taken to address the situation or task. There is a focus on what was done to accomplish the goal. *Result*: Here all aspects of results are articulated that show direct correlations to the outcomes of the actions taken.

This book jointly provides theoretical and empirical contributions in a monographic way to give an overall view of the main issues and methods in brand licensing. It also provides useful insights for practitioners and managers in the fields at the forefront of licensing strategy and management. Finally, the text provides tools and solutions, including case studies, for effectively implementing long-lasting brand licensing programs. This book intends to be a valuable guide for postgraduate students, MBAs and executive education. It can be adopted as a textbook in brand management courses and masters in the following subdisciplines: Strategy, Brand Management, Marketing, B2B Marketing, Export Strategy, International Business, Product Strategy and Trade. Students and executives should be involved in brand expansion, brand extension and licensing strategy within the areas of brand strategy, marketing, communication, export strategy and trade. The book also reaches out to the interest of consultants and practicing executives working in automotive, communication, entertainment, fashion, sports, toys and other industry sectors – whose roles and responsibilities deal with the critical issues related to brand strategy, brand expansion and licensing. They can find appropriate answers and useful insights to their questions concerning how to manage the licensing process and how to select licensees and licensors to determine the categories to expand and improve the overall effectiveness of the program. Another potential audience of this book are scholars interested in brand strategy and product strategy.

The book consists of five chapters. Chapter 1 examines how the world of licensing works providing a general overview of the main aspects related to brand licensing programs. This topic is analyzed, focusing on strategic issues related to design, implementation and execution of a brand licensing program. In particular, the first three sections analyze what makes licensing programs fail or succeed. Section 4 describes the different types of licensing including corporate, character, music, sports and technology. Section 5 introduces how licensing is used in digital platforms, and Section 6 discusses how IP is managed in the digital world. The chapter concludes with the analysis of three case studies reflecting on the opportunity and limitations of digital brand licensing.

Chapter 2 is about charting the path for enduring licensing programs. Section 1 explores the current state of brand licensing, highlighting its distinctive assets whose value lies in the reputation, image, quality and stylistic standards associated with the brand. Sections 2, 3 and 4 consider the strategic value of brand licensing in looking at the licensor and licensee perspective. Sections 5, 6 and 7 provide some examples of enduring partnership which involve, respectively, licensees, agents and multi-level licenses. Section 8 examines the brand licensing process steps for building long-term successful programs. Section 9 displays an example of a successful long-term brand licensing program in the field of sport.

Chapter 3 examines the key issue of how to create value through brand licensing strategy. It is focused on the valuable brand components needed for crafting a licensing program and on the metrics to use for evaluating the brand growth and its abilities to expand. Section 1 depicts the importance of brand positioning in choosing the category and the partners to be involved in the program. Section 2 concerns how to define the brand positioning statement, how to identify the key elements of the brand architecture and how to analyze the points of parity and points of difference between the brand and its competitors. Section 3 is focused on brand growth to unlock licensing latent value distinguishing between brand extension, brand expansion and brand internationalization. Section 4 is about how to measure the power of the brand to be license-able. Section 5 provides an example of a brand growth in multiple directions starting from extension to expansion into new categories.

Chapter 4 explores how to execute a brand licensing program. It begins with choosing the licensor according to the LASSO (Lateral, Addictive, Storied, Scalable and Ownable) Method. Section 2 details how to choose the licensee based on an assessment check. Section 3 lists the components of a brand licensing program. Section 4 provides tools including destination metrics, application and projections, due diligence, deal terms alignment, contract negotiation, licensing contract and deal memo, orientation session, business plan and monitoring and core program elements. Section 5 gives a best-in-class example of executing a brand licensing program where the licensor and the licensee are committed to an agreement that lasts for 100 years.

Finally, Chapter 5 addresses the issue that not all licensing programs are successful. Some of them end with financial loss or damage to the brand's business. This chapter concludes with the most frequent pitfalls to avoid when operating a licensing agreement. Section 1 recognizes the mistakes most encountered with the licensing partner and suggests how to deal with them. Section 2 highlights the risk-taking and the risk-mitigation that characterize licensing programs. Section 3 illustrates how a case where these pitfalls can be avoided and overcome in order to create value and an enduring brand licensing program.

References

Araz, O. M., Choi, T. M., Olson, D. L., & Salman, F. S. (2020). Data analytics for operational risk management. *Decision Sciences, 51*(6), 1316–1319.

Börjeson, N., & Boström, M. (2018). Towards reflexive responsibility in a textile supply chain. *Business Strategy and the Environment, 27*(2), 230–239.

Brand Licensing Market Report 2023–2031. (2023). *Business research insights*. www.businessresearchinsights.com/enquiry/queries/100200

Canalichio, P. (2019). *Grow brand value while accelerating revenue growth*. Entrepreneur Media.

Cardinali, S., Travaglini, M., & Giovannetti, M. (2019). Increasing brand orientation and brand capabilities using licensing: An opportunity for SMES in international markets. *Journal of the Knowledge Economy, 10*, 1808–1830.

Chernev, A. (2020). *Strategic brand management*. Cerebellum Press.

Christensen, H. B., & Nikolaev, V. V. (2013). Does fair value accounting for non-financial assets pass the market test? *Review of Accounting Studies, 18*, 734–775.

Desai, D. R. (2012). From trademarks to brands. *Florida Law Review, 64*, 981.

Gibson, J. (2006). Risk aversion and rights accretion in intellectual property law. *Yale Law Journal, 116*, 882.

Goldscheider, R., & Gordon, A. H. (Eds.). (2006). *Licensing best practices: Strategic, territorial, and technology issues*. John Wiley & Sons.

Gupta, S., Gallear, D., Rudd, J., & Foroudi, P. (2020). The impact of brand value on brand competitiveness. *Journal of Business Research, 112,* 210–222.

Heath, T. B., DelVecchio, D., & McCarthy, M. S. (2011). The asymmetric effects of extending brands to lower and higher quality. *Journal of Marketing, 75*(4), 3–20.

Joshi, R., & Yadav, R. (2019). The study of brand extension among generation Y in the Indian market. *International Journal of Indian Culture and Business Management, 19*(3), 339–353.

Kirca, A. H., Randhawa, P., Talay, M. B., & Akdeniz, M. B. (2020). The interactive effects of product and brand portfolio strategies on brand performance: Longitudinal evidence from the US automotive industry. *International Journal of Research in Marketing, 37*(2), 421–439.

Parr, R. (2007). *Royalty rates for licensing intellectual property.* John Wiley & Sons.

Pina, J. M., Iversen, N. M., & Martinez, E. (2010). Feedback effects of brand extensions on the brand image of global brands: A comparison between Spain and Norway. *Journal of Marketing Management, 26*(9–10), 943–966.

Raugust, K. (2004). *The licensing business handbook.* EPM Communications.

Sadgrove, K. (2016). *The complete guide to business risk management.* Routledge.

Sáiz, P., & Castro, R. (2018). Trademarks in branding: Legal issues and commercial practices. *Business History, 60*(8), 1105–1126.

Salinas, E. M., & Pérez, J. M. P. (2009). Modeling the brand extensions' influence on brand image. *Journal of Business Research, 62*(1), 50–60.

Sherman, A. (2011). *Franchising and licensing: Two powerful ways to grow your business in any economy.* Amacom/Harper Collins.

Somaya, D., Kim, Y., & Vonortas, N. S. (2011). Exclusivity in licensing alliances: Using hostages to support technology commercialization. *Strategic Management Journal, 32*(2), 159–186.

Steenkamp, J. B. (2017). *Global brand strategy: World-wise marketing in the age of branding.* Springer Nature.

1

THE WORLD OF LICENSING

Learning Objectives

The aim of the chapter is to provide content and tools to answer the following questions: What are the main characteristics of the world of licensing, what makes licensing programs fail or succeed, how Media Digital Licensing can be used to create value for brand owners and how intellectual program management matters in digital licensing? After reading this chapter, the readers will understand the strategic importance of brand licensing both for licensors and for licensees. They will be able to identify different types of licensing, assess their value and analyze their trends across product categories, markets and channels. Finally, the readers will be able to critically discuss issues concerning the factors that make brand licensing successful or that can cause its failure.

Keywords: Brand, Licensing Strategy, Types of Brand Licensing, Licensing Programs Failure and Success, Media Digital Licensing, Intellectual Property in Digital Platforms.

1. Introduction to the World of Brand Licensing

Brand licensing is the relationship involving a brand lending itself to a third-party manufacturer in a particular category in exchange for royalty revenue payments typically as a percentage of net sales. An arrangement to license a brand requires a licensing agreement (Nimmer & Dodd, 2005). A licensing agreement authorizes a company that markets a product or service (a licensee) to lease or rent a brand from a brand owner who operates a licensing program (a licensor). From a strategic perspective, brand licensing can be defined as an agreement that authorizes a company that markets a product or service (a licensee) to lease or rent a brand from a brand owner who operates a licensing program (a licensor) in return for a portion of the sales revenue (royalty). Brand licensing is a strategy used by companies to extract value from their brand through the temporary concession of the rights deriving from the brand to third parties. The licensor, that is, the company owning the brand, grants the licensee the right to use the brand

DOI: 10.4324/9781003364566-2

in its own products or to sell items with the licensor's brand upon payment of a royalty. For the licensor, brand licensing represents a tool to monetize the brand indirectly (Jayachandran et al., 2013).

From a strategic point of view, there are a variety of reasons to license a brand. Licensing offers a means to expand its use and penetrate new markets without direct investment in production plants and distribution channels. If the brand has a high preference, licensing enables the brand owner or licensor to unlock the brand's latent value and satisfy pent-up demand. Through licensing, the licensor has the ability to enter new categories practically overnight, gaining an immediate brand presence on store shelves and often in the media. Brand licensing also enables licensors to try out potential new businesses or geographical markets with a relatively small upfront risk. By licensing a brand to a third-party manufacturer, the licensor can try new businesses, or move into new countries with a smaller upfront investment than by building and staffing its own operations. An additional benefit for the licensor is to increase customer brand loyalty.

For the licensee, that is, the one who uses the license, this type of contract represents an opportunity to enter new businesses quickly and with a moderate risk. The licensee can leverage the notoriety and reputation of an existing brand to target new markets or niches of consumers. People may wonder how Coca-Cola, a company so focused on meeting their beverage needs, sells Coca-Cola branded tee shirts or caps, or how Rubbermaid provides such a range of products under a single brand name. While companies sometimes manufacture these items themselves, at other times, they may choose to allow a manufacturer to produce and market these products under their brand names. In return for the use of their brand, these companies charge the manufacturer a fee.

Licensing means the renting or leasing of an intangible asset, which includes a song, such as Need You Now by Lady Antebellum, a character like Disney's Donald Duck, a person's name such as George Clooney or a brand like The Ritz-Carlton. This book is focused on strategic brand licensing, which is characterized by a commitment and involvement of both the licensor and the licensee in the production and distribution of the licensed brand that lasts in the medium and long term. An example of strategic brand licensing is that of Caterpillar. The program is active in over 150 countries and generates $3 billion in licensed product sales at retail. The program has allowed Caterpillar to build a direct-to-consumer connection for over 30 years while building on its core equity of toughness in a variety of categories (Canalichio, 2018).

Strategic brand licensing is a way to create value both for the licensor and the licensee by exploiting the intangible assets over time. The licensor has the opportunity to extend its brand into new product categories, expanding product portfolios, targets, distribution channels and geographic areas with a limited investment compared to a direct one. The licensee expands its product range, leveraging the strength of the licensor's brand, reputation and image, thus enhancing its market positioning. Investing in enduring partnerships is of strategic importance for both firms and industry, and requires a deep knowledge and understanding of the art of licensing management.

The Global Licensing Industry is an expanding industry with a strong presence in all regions with a particular growth by absolute and percentage in the online channel. By region, the 2022 retail sales of licensed products and services were as follows: US/Canada $203B (59.6%), W Europe $63B (18.5%), N Asia $32B (9.3%), LATAM $14B (4.1%), SE

Asia/PAC $12B (3.7%), E Europe $11B (3.1%) and ME/Africa $6B (1.6%). The world-wide percentage of online sales across all regions dropped from 34% to 30% from 2021 to 2022 while Brick & Mortar (B&M) sales grew from 66 percent to 70 percent. The greatest growth in online sales occurred in the Middle East and Africa, where it increased from 15 percent to 17 percent. All the other regions either dropped or remained the same (2023 Global Licensing Industry Study).

Worldwide retail sales of licensed products and services have been increasing over the last five years and have seen a growth rate of 8.0 percent from 2021 to 2022. The value of 2021 was $315.5 billion. Product categories that enabled consumers to use their favorite brands to reintroduce fun and excitement back into their lives outside the home saw significant success. This led to the licensing industry again migrating with the tastes of the consumer – mainly to the property categories of Sports, Music, Collegiate and Corporate. These licensed property sectors showed strength in 2022 by participating in product categories like services in the hospitality, travel and entertainment sectors; location-based events and promotions; sporting goods; lawn, garden and outdoor products; food and beverage; casino gaming; gifts; fashion accessories; footwear; and health & beauty. Entertainment and Characters represent the highest retail revenue (4.5%) followed by the Corporate Brands (25.7%). From 2021 to 2022, Music (26.1%), No Profit (25.6%) and Sports (19.50%) showed the greatest growth, while Publishing saw a dramatic decrease (−13.4%) after growing 28% from 2019 to 2021. The year 2022 was therefore categorized by strong growth in product categories resulting from out-of-home leisure activities with Location-Based Entertainment/Promotions (+67.3%), Licensed Services including Restaurants, Hotels, Travel and Hospitality (+205.6%), and Casino Gaming/Lotteries (+19.1%) – all showing very strong growth during the year.

Overall, 2022 was a strong year for the industry with more than an 8 percent growth in global sales of licensed merchandise and services versus the prior year. With the drastic increase in foot traffic at retail also came an increase of in-store impulse buys that are crucial to licensed product sales. For 2023 consumers will expect a seamless shopping experience across channels in the upcoming year. But because of the inflationary period of 2022, consumers will be significantly more price-conscious, making customers more likely to shift from channel to channel to make their retail purchases, powered by peer recommendations and price comparison. Beyond brand loyalty, several factors will become increasingly important for brand owners, licensees and retailers. Two-thirds of retail executives expect price to be more important than brand or retailer loyalty in 2023. Additionally, young consumers have far greater expectations for companies to uphold and foster high ESG (environmental, social and governance) and DEI (diversity, equity and inclusion) standards. Three-quarters of Gen Z consumers surveyed said sustainability was more important than brand when making a purchase decision (Deloitte, 2023; Retail Industry Outlook). Ensuring that the consumer experience is at the heart of investments in brands, products and channels will be the key to prosperity in our industry for the foreseeable future.

ORIGINS OF LICENSING

The origin of brand licensing, understood as the use of names or characters on products other than the original ones, dates back to the late 1920s and 1930s in the US. They are related to motion pictures, toys and comics. In the 1930s, licensing spread rapidly with comic books; comic strips used a variety of types of licensed merchandise including tee shirts, hats, sunglasses, cups, postcards, magnets, key chains, posters, pens or pins to connect consumers with their favorite characters. For example, Walt Disney in 1928 introduced the first license granting the use of an image of Mickey Mouse for a school diary. With the invention of television, consumers were further connected with brands. For example, the Mickey Mouse character started to expand further into licensed merchandise when people fell in love with the character. Today, The Walt Disney Company is a dominant consumer product goods company with 2,100 characters as of 2023 (www.FeaturedAnimation.com). Much, if not all of their products sold, are officially licensed merchandise.

In the 1950s many other companies, including French houses from Pierrre Cardin to Givenchy and Charles Jourdan, sought to exploit the opportunity coming from market demand (Chevalier & Mazzalovo, 2008). They saw that consumers wanted merchandise integrated with the specific characters they liked. To start, manufacturers developed relationships with brand owners to enable merchandise that consumers wanted to buy. Brand licensing grew as the market expanded over time. A good example can be that of TGI Fridays, which is a very successful restaurant chain. TGI Fridays is so popular that consumers want to buy frozen food branded TGI Fridays at their supermarket (Brody & Lord, 2007). TGI Fridays developed a partnership with a frozen food supplier who had a relationship with a supermarket to produce TGI Fridays appetizers, entrees or desserts.

2. What Makes Licensing Programs Fail

With a market size of over $340 billion globally, brand licensing today has a profound influence on the competitive strategies of companies. Many sectors are involved, including sports, apparel, CPGs, technology, digital, Metaverse, music, entertainment and art. Yet, entering positions within the $340-billion Global Licensing Industry are not enough. Many brand licensing programs fail (Cowen & Crampton, 2002; Meschnig et al., 2023). The types of failures fall into the following categories:

- Choosing the incorrect category in which to expand.
- Selecting the wrong company to execute the licensing program.
- Not ensuring the licensee can perform the job.
- Negotiating unsustainable values for the terms in the licensing agreement.
- Having a flawed licensing agreement without the proper guidelines or protections.
- Failing to orientate the licensee on how to engage with the licensor.
- Not requiring the licensee to establish a business plan to govern the program.

Choosing the Incorrect Category in Which to Expand

The real challenge is to strike the right balance between surprise, whereby the brand appears where it was not expected, and alignment, whereby the appearance of the brand in this sector makes sense because it mirrors what the brand already means. If the association is too lateral, or if the brand isn't strong enough, the whole arrangement simply looks fetching. There are many examples of brand expansions that have gone terribly wrong: BiC's 1998 venture into perfume in the US (Michel & Donthu, 2014) or disposable pantyhose in

Greece, Austria and Ireland (Rotfeld, 2008). Consumers didn't *get it* and the extensions ultimately failed. In a nutshell, this means there needs to be a clear line of sight between what the brand says and stands for, and everywhere that it is seen. These associations can be literal or emotive, as long as they are well-thought-out. They stem from a brand's expansion point. The expansion point is the common reference point for every place that the brand moves into and also is the singular idea that relates consumers to the brand (Canalichio, 2018). Two questions are pertinent here. First, how does the addition expand on what consumers know about the brand already? Second, where can that expansion take the brand next? Each addition is like a station on a rail network, carrying the traveler further from the point they started from, and yet linked back to that starting point intuitively and effortlessly.

Selecting the Wrong Company to Execute the Licensing Program

If the licensee does not possess the skills, capabilities or resources to create the licensed merchandise at a sufficiently high standard, then the consumer either will not purchase the licensed product or be disappointed with the product when they do. This will cause the licensing program to fail. When the Stanley brand chose to expand their brand via licensing, Stanley decided to utilize a licensing agency to manage their program. However, the agency failed to understand Stanley's brand positioning or standards. It signed licensing agreements with a variety of companies for the portable fan, desk organizer and Christmas lights timer categories. The licensees did not possess the capability of making products that met Stanley's standards (Stone & Trebbien, 2019). Ultimately the licensed products sold by these companies in the marketplace created a misunderstanding of what the Stanley brand stood for and meant to consumers. The brand extensions did not incorporate the Stanley brand attributes, causing a disconnect between the brand and the consumer, harming the brand. The results were devastating and Stanley had to exit the categories. Later, Stanley's agency improved the licensee selection process and their new licensees built the brand's attributes into the design and manufacturing process, creating superb licensed products that found success in the marketplace.

When choosing a licensee, the licensor and its agency should consider the following parameters:

- Market share in the product category.
- Size and financial strength.
- Current or previous licenses held.
- Awards received.
- Consumer perception.

Not Ensuring the Licensee Can Perform the Job

Often licensors select companies to be their licensees which have superior product development and operational expertise. These licensees, however, often do not have marketing capability or a distribution network. They would be better suited as an Original Equipment Manufacturer (OEM). The brand owner could then build these sourced products into their portfolio and sell them into their distribution network. Instead, the licensee struggles to build demand or get the licensed products into the market. As a result, the licensee does not achieve its committed sales targets and is required to pay the minimum guaranteed royalties. Ultimately, the licensee will seek allowances and the license will fail. To avoid this type of failure, the licensee could have a strong leadership, a financial strength, a marketing acumen and an operational capability (Martensen, 2003).

Negotiating Unsustainable Values for the Terms in the Licensing Agreement

Sometimes a licensee can desire a license with a brand so much that it will agree to values for the terms in the licensing agreement that are unachievable or unsustainable. These often include minimum guaranteed royalties it cannot afford to pay, licensed merchandise sales targets that are impossible to reach, annual new product development amounts that exceed their capabilities or quality standards they cannot achieve. When this happens, the licensee will be in default with their contract terms. At this point, the licensor is forced to agree to lower targets or to terminate the agreement. To avoid failure, both parties should ensure the deal terms are achievable and sustainable. While each party inherently desires the most favorable terms for their company, the best set of deal terms are those that allow both parties to achieve a successful long-term licensing program. A successful licensor must keep the end in mind and practice win-win negotiating strategies. If the licensee does not believe the terms are equitable, the agreement will fail. Savvy licensees will have identified several choices of brands in which to acquire a license and will set internal limits on what deal terms they will accept, regardless of the brand. Assuming that both parties agree on the terms of the contract, the deal terms are acknowledged in writing and then passed to an attorney to place into a licensing agreement template. This template should include all other terms and conditions (such as Confidential Information Representations and Warranties).

Having a Flawed Licensing Agreement without the Proper Guidelines or Protections

When the licensing agreement fails to articulate clearly the approval process or the brand's visual identity standards, the licensee risks products that could be disapproved. These products fail to incorporate the brand's attributes into the design of the licensed products. This lack of approval can have a cascading negative impact on the licensee's business as they will be unable to get their product into the marketplace (Nimmer & Dodd, 2005). Some ways to prevent this from happening are to ensure the licensee has a full understanding of the Brand Positioning, Promise and Architecture. A licensing program with a clear approval process should give clear direction on details, such as the placement of the logo on the product, how it is affixed and the material from where it is constructed. Additionally, the licensor should ensure the licensee has a copy of the brand style guide so they have the required information to create concepts that will be approved and that represent the brand accurately.

Failing to Orientate the Licensee on How to Engage with the Licensor

The execution of the contract signifies the beginning of the relationship. Without a proper orientation, the licensee will not be optimally familiarized with the licensor's brand and the overall licensing program (Wiedmann & Ludewig, 2008). Moreover, the licensor will not gain the information it needs to be successful. Orientation provides opportunities for key members of both parties to meet, get to know one another, and review expectations and contractual requirements. Without this knowledge, there often can be misunderstandings and unfamiliarity by the licensor regarding the staff and resources dedicated to the program, the Product Forecast, the Marketing Plan and the Product Concepts. Similarly, the licensee will lack familiarity and expectations regarding the Brand Architecture, the Brand Positioning, the Category Positioning, the Timelines, the Key Terms, the Review of Testing and Audit Protocol, the Approval Process and the Licensing Style Guide. These often lead to brand licensing program inefficiencies and failures.

Not Requiring the Licensee to Establish a Business Plan to Govern the Program

The Business Planning phase defines what gets measured. When a licensor is incapable of accurately monitoring the licensee's business, it cannot ensure the program will be successful (Bass, 2004). Moreover, if the licensor cannot ensure the licensee has set achievable targets, it will be unable to maximize the license. These misunderstandings can be superseded with a good orientation program, but without it, both parties will lack understanding which will undermine the licensing program. To avoid this type of failure, the licensee should develop a one-year business plan that is founded on the licensor's Brand and Category Positioning Statements. The business plan should also include any Minimum Sales terms, Minimum Guaranteed Royalties and the royalty rate. With these incorporated, the licensee should develop an accurate forecast and set realistic goals. Projected royalties can then be calculated by the licensee based on the sales projections and reviewed against the minimum guaranteed royalties to assess the robustness of their business plan. The business plan must be appropriately structured to allow the licensor and the licensee to work together in a seamless partnership that enables the plan to be successful.

EXAMPLES OF BRAND LICENSING AND EXPANSION FAILURES

Table 1.1 illustrates several examples of brand licensing and expansion failures. We selected the cases in which well-known companies developed a brand licensing agreement with a licensee and the failure is limited to the agreement and not to the brand overall. We considered failure as a reduction or decline in revenue over time. We identify the following reasons that explain why the expansion disappeared from the market, that are low financial outcomes, for example, not enough sales or profit; the creation of brand confusion that is not aligned with the brand's positioning; a lack of connection between the brand's core products; and the category in which it was licensed.

TABLE 1.1 Brand Extension – Reason for Failure

Brand	Brand Extension – Reason for Failure
BiC Underwear	BiC is a company based out of France that is best known for making ballpoint pens. In 1998 BiC extended their brand into disposable women's underwear, a product category completely unrelated to anything they had made before. The idea behind the disposable underwear was that BiC had been very successful in making disposable pens, lighters and razors, so why not make an underwear that women could use once and then throw away. The product met an early demise when it was taken off the shelves in early 1999. The main reason for failure for this extension is brand confusion.

Brand	Brand Extension – Reason for Failure
Cheeto Lip Balm	Frito Lay tried to expand into the lip balm product category in 2005 by launching Cheeto lip balm. The idea was that Cheeto lovers could experience the Cheeto taste even when they weren't eating the delicious snack. The product got many negative reviews as consumers could not wrap their minds around a cheese snack-flavored lip balm. The main reason for failure for this extension is brand confusion.
Cocaine the Energy Drink	In 2006 Redux Beverage Company created an energy drink and named it Cocaine Energy drink and had the tagline "The Legal Alternative." Along with the controversy that came with the choice of name, the energy drink also caused health concerns for many consumers. Cocaine energy drink contained 350 percent more stimulants than the popular energy Red Bull. Because of the association with an illegal drug and the unhealthy ingredients, Cocaine Energy drink became a quick failure. The main reason for failure for this extension is unclear brand positioning.
Colgate Kitchen Entrees	Colgate is a brand that is known for selling oral hygiene products such as toothpastes, toothbrushes, mouthwashes and dental floss. Colgate created Colgate Kitchen Entrees in 1982 with the idea that one would eat Colgate Frozen dinners and then brush their teeth with Colgate toothpaste. Along with entering the very saturated frozen food market, consumers did not make a connection and in a lot of cases were disgusted by the idea of Colgate food, leading to a complete brand extension failure. The main reason for failure for this extension is due to a lack of connection between the brand's core products and the category in which it was licensed resulting in brand confusion.
Cosmopolitan Yogurt	Cosmopolitan is considered an international fashion magazine that also features some sexy articles. Cosmopolitan is published in 36 languages and distributed in more than 100 countries. The link between a magazine and yogurt was made when a study in 1999 showed that over 65 percent of people used edible products in the bedroom. Along with consumers not seeing the connection between the two, the yogurt was pricier than its competitor and was off the shelves less than 18 months after launching. The main reason for failure for this extension is a lack of connection between the brand's core products and the category in which it was licensed.
Harley Davidson Perfume	Harley Davidson is an American motorcycle manufacturer that has an extremely loyal brand following around the world. Many consumers consider the Harley Davidson brand to be a lifestyle and have a long-term relationship with the brand. While the motorcycle family has been successful in extending its brand into apparel, even the most loyal consumers did not see the connection between a high-powered motorcycle and perfume. The main reason for failure for this extension is a lack of connection between the brand's core products and the category in which it was licensed.

(Continued)

TABLE 1.1 (Continued)

Brand	Brand Extension – Reason for Failure
Coors Spring Water	The Coors Brewing Company is known for its Pilsner-style beer but tried to tap into the growing bottled water market in 1990. However, many consumers were thrown off by the bottle having the same Coors logo font and label as the beer bottles. This made people worry about drinking it or giving it to their children because of the association of alcohol. The main reason for failure for this extension is brand confusion.
Evian Water Bras	Evian is a brand specializing and well-known for bottling mineral water that expanded into the female undergarment category by creating the Evian Water Bra. The bra contained a pocket that was meant to be filled with water, preferably Evian mineral water. The bra was marketed to consumers as a solution for "humid breasts." The main reason for failure for this extension is a lack of connection between the brand's core products and the category in which it was licensed.
Life Savers Soda	Lifesavers is an American brand of ring-shaped hard candy. In the 1980s Lifesavers developed a soda that came in the five flavors of the hard candy. Despite doing well in taste tests before the launch, the soda was taken off the shelves shortly after because consumers just were not interested in the idea of drinking liquid candy. The main reason for failure for this extension is a lack of connection between the brand's core products and the category in which it was licensed.
Smith and Wesson Bike	Gun Manufacturer Smith and Wesson has been making police bicycles for about 20 years. In 2002 the company tried to sell mountain bikes to the public. The Smith and Wesson Mountain bike became a brand extension failure as consumers did not associate a gun company with biking. The main reason for failure for this extension is brand confusion.
Thirsty Dog! Water	In the early 1990s, the Original Pet Drink Company based out of Ft. Lauderdale Florida developed a water bottle that contained flavored water for dogs and eventually cats. The flavors of the water were supposed to be appetizing to pets with flavors such as beef, chicken etc. This product was considered a failure when many pet owners did not want to spend the extra money on a pricey flavored bottle of water for their pets. Some pet owners also questioned the nutritional value of artificially flavored water versus good old H20. The main reason for this extension is low financial outcomes, e.g., not enough sales or profit due to a large enough target audience. This category might achieve financial success in today's market.
Trump University	In 2005 Donald Trump started Trump University, which was an American for-profit education company that ran a real estate training program. The organization was not an accredited university and did not offer college credits, degrees or grades to its students. Many students of Trump University claimed they had been taken advantage of and lawsuits started to pile up against the university. In 2010 Trump University closed its doors. The main reason for this extension is low financial outcomes, e.g., not enough sales or profit due to the lack of selection of a suitable licensing partner.

3. What Makes Licensing Programs Succeed

A strong brand and tailor-made licensing program can increase the likelihood of successful partnerships (Sherman, 2011). Several variables that help ensure brand licensing programs succeed include: a brand licensing process aligned with the brand and consistent with its brand's positioning; a brand having the potential to expand into new markets and categories, and a strong connection between the brand's core products and the category in which it was licensed; a licensee capable of executing the license; a licensing agreement with terms that enable both parties to meet their business objectives over the long term; and a licensing agreement that ensures a collaborative and mutually beneficial approach.

A brand licensing process employed by the brand owner is strengthened if it is aligned with the brand and consistent with its brand's positioning (Colucci et al., 2008). The brand owner supports the program organizationally, has an infrastructure in place to facilitate approvals of products and services, and integrates the licensee into its go-to-market strategy to ensure a seamless transition.

A brand increases the potential of expanding into new markets and categories, if there exists a strong connection between the brand's core products and the category in which it was licensed. It possesses high top-of-mind brand awareness when a category is mentioned, which means consumers must name it when asked which brands are best in its class. The brand commands consumer loyalty and is therefore something that customers do not want to be without. Consumers understand the brand and embrace what it stands for. Finally, the brand achieves superior business results in its margin, sales growth and expandability.

A licensee which is capable of executing the license under several conditions. The licensee is financially strong with best-in-class products that meet pent-up consumer demand. Its products are sold into the channels and regions where they intend to sell the licensed product. The licensee possesses the capability of building the licensed brand's essence into their products (Progoff & Palladino, 2005). Finally, the licensee has the ability to invest a minimum of three percent of its net sales generated from the brand licensing program into marketing the product.

The terms of a licensing agreement should allow both parties to meet their business objectives over the long term, generating high financial outcomes, for example, strong sales or profit. In every licensing contract, there are certain deal terms that define the structure of the contract. The deal terms include such parameters as the term of the contract, where the licensed products will be sold, what royalty rate will be paid and what trademarks will be used. Because the value of these terms will be unique to every licensing contract, they must be negotiated between the licensor and the licensee (Haigh & Knowles, 2004). While each party inherently wants to arrive at the most favorable terms for their side, the best set of deal terms are those that allow both parties to achieve a successful long-term licensing program.

A licensing agreement where both parties take a collaborative and mutually beneficial approach in working together makes the program successful. The relationship is based on trust and respect. Moreover, the licensor and the licensee value each other's expertise, opinions and contributions. This allows them to have open and effective communication. They listen attentively and communicate their thoughts and concerns effectively. The licensor and the licensee also have shared goals and vision. They align their objectives and work together to achieve them, ensuring that everyone understands and is committed to the shared purpose.

EXAMPLES OF SUCCESSFUL BRAND LICENSING PROGRAMS

Table 1.2 reports a few examples of successful brand licensing programs (Santo, 2015). These programs have benefited from several factors that have led to their enduring success. They include: a strong brand licensing process from the brand owner consistently with a brand alignment with the brand's positioning; the brand's potential to expand into new markets and categories, and consequently a strong connection between the brand's core products and the category in which it was licensed; competence of the licensee in executing the license; favorable licensing agreement terms to meet both parties' business objectives over the long term, generating high financial outcomes, for example, strong sales or profit; and the commitment toward the partnership both from the licensor and the licensee. The examples show that building a successful brand licensing program requires an effort both of the licensor and of the licensee to leverage many variables.

TABLE 1.2 Brand Extension – Reason for Success

Brand	Brand Extension – Reason for Success
Better Homes and Garden	Meredith has a license with Walmart for Better Homes and Gardens home goods. The license works because the core brand, Better Homes & Gardens (BH&G) magazine, and the licensed category (home goods) are both focused on the needs of the next generation of homeowners. Walmart had a flourishing backyard furniture business but wanted to shift indoors. The tie-in with BH&G enabled them to reach out to house-proud consumers and find new ways to fall in love with their home again. The success of that initiative enabled BH&G to cultivate new product lines with new customers. The arrangement helped Walmart to change the conversation they have with this consumer group from one focused on the practicality of polyester to one based on aesthetics and entertainment. It also helped BH&G by enabling consumers to make decisions in-store that enable them to bring their desired lifestyle home in order for their home to look more like the magazine. The main reason for the success of this extension is related to the commitment between the partnership from both the licensor and the licensee.
Winnie the Pooh	In 1930 Stephen Slesinger purchased the US and Canadian merchandising, television, recording and other rights from A.A. Milne's Winnie the Pooh character. He began to promote the bear and create merchandise for sale. Within a year the loveable bear was a $50-million business, that is, almost $700 million in today's dollars. Slesinger would go on to license Pooh and his friends for the next three decades, creating a panoply of Pooh dolls, records, board games, puzzles and films, before the rights were acquired in 1961 by The Walt Disney Company.

Brand	Brand Extension – Reason for Success
	Today, Winnie the Pooh is known in virtually every country and literally thousands of different Pooh products have been manufactured under license, generating billions of dollars in revenue. The main reasons for the success of this extension are the brand's potential to expand into new markets and categories, and consequently a strong connection between the brand's core products and the category in which it was licensed and favorable licensing agreement terms to meet both parties' business objectives over the long term, generating high financial outcomes, e.g., strong sales or profit.
Star Wars	In 1977 Marc Pevers headed up the licensing section for 20th Century Fox, which held the rights to the Star Wars brand. Pevers needed to be able to show the film to prospective licensees to stimulate sales, but George Lucas, the producer, insisted on secrecy. In Pevers' experience, small companies that had limited resources tried to extract as much revenue from their license as possible by producing licensed products to meet their most favorable projections. This offer saturated the market with too much licensed product. Pevers promoted the film at the 1977 Toy Fair. Bernard Loomis, who ran Kenner Toys, was interested. Kenner ensured there was a uniform look and packaging. Pevers recalls that Kenner was willing to not overproduce, enabling the company to have sustained sales over a long period. Kenner sold 50,000 figure sets in the first run. Sales of Kenner's Star Wars action figures reached 40 million units in 1978, accounting for revenue of $100 million. To put that in perspective, that same year Fox grossed $40 million in total royalty revenue from all its other releases. Total box office revenues for the original six Star Wars motion pictures would go on to exceed $5 billion, putting the series right up there with James Bond and Harry Potter. For many studios at the time licensing was a side business to help drive awareness of the real hero, which was the release itself. Any consumer products licensing revenue was considered gravy. The main reasons for the success of this extension include the competence of the licensee in executing the license and favorable licensing agreement terms to meet both parties' business objectives over the long term, generating high financial outcomes, e.g., strong sales or profit.
Caterpillar	Founded in the late 1800s, Caterpillar today is approximately a $60-billion company that makes large dirt-moving products for farming and construction around the globe. These products are sold B2B and have a high price point. Caterpillar, whose brand is known for ruggedness and reliability, leveraged its brand through licensing to connect with consumers around the world. The brand licensing program enabled Caterpillar to partner with some great companies that have done a lot to build the brand in their respective categories. Thirty years ago, when Caterpillar started, they asked what kind of products a tractor owner needed to do their job. They entered safety shoes, work wear and eye protection. The company was able to cross over.

(Continued)

TABLE 1.2 (Continued)

Brand	Brand Extension – Reason for Success
	After marketing analysis, Caterpillar became aware that the consumer wanted them to extend their brand into new categories. Today the Caterpillar brand licensing program sells almost $3 billion of merchandise in dozens of categories globally. According to Kenny Beaupre, Caterpillar Brand Licensing Manager, "Anyone can slap a logo on anything. What has been successful for us is when we have used our brand and marketed our brand attributes – to the strength, to the durability, to the quality, to the rugged, to the tough. Whenever we have stayed close to our core attributes, that's when we have had success." The main reasons for the success of this extension are the brand's potential to expand into new markets and categories, a strong connection between the brand's core products and the category in which it was licensed and a strong brand licensing process from the brand owner consistently with a brand alignment with the brand's positioning.

4. Brand Licensing Categories

There are different types of brand licensing that are normally seen (Batra et al., 2010). On the basis of the theme and area covered they are classified into: Corporate Licensing, Character Licensing, Fashion Licensing, Technology Licensing, Art Licensing, Music Licensing, Celebrity Licensing and Sports Licensing. Table 1.3 lists some examples of the licensing categories in the global marketplace today.

Corporate Licensing includes corporate brands like Crayola, LEGO and Sephora. Corporate Licensing helps corporate brands expand into new territories that could have been impossible to penetrate without licensing programs, which enable the brand to stay true to the idea for which they are renowned (Laforet & Saunders, 2005). Through Corporate Licensing, the licensor grants the licensee the right to produce goods or services using the licensor's know-how and to distribute and label the products with the licensor's trademark. An example of this is Coca-Cola partnering with the Nagano Olympic Committee (co-licensor), Aminco, a pin company, and other licensees to produce Coca-Cola Nagano Olympic trading pins, apparel, plush and commemorative bottles to sell. Without licensing with the Nagano Olympic Committee and the program licensees, the opportunity to expand the brand in this area and sell millions of dollars of merchandise likely would have been lost.

The second type of licensing is *Character Licensing*. At the 2022 International Licensing Expo in Las Vegas, Character Licensing was a dominant topic at the show (Crombar, 2023). In attendance were Disney, Marvel and Warner Brothers, which own some of the most highly sought-after character brands when we think of Character Licensing. It is these character brands that consumers know and want on a variety of cherished products. Character brands are extremely popular which has enticed businesses to want these brands on their products (Hosany et al., 2013). Licensing with character brands helps businesses connect with the consumers and grab that associative imagery of those characters to make

TABLE 1.3 Examples of Licensing Categories

Licensing – Categories	Examples
Character	Barbie, Bluey, Simpsons
Fashion	H&M, Nike, Tommy Hilfiger
Technology	IBM, Microsoft, Sony
Art	Thomas Kinkaid, Katina Zinner, Somerset
Music	Apple Music, Spotify, Amazon
Celebrity	George Clooney, Queen Elizabeth II, Lady Gaga
Sports	Valentino Rossi, Lebron James, Lionel Messi
Corporate	Crayola, LEGO, Sephora

their brands more exciting. For instance, Doraemon is a Japanese manga series written and illustrated by Fujiko F. Fujio. The manga was first serialized in December 1969, with its 1,345 individual chapters compiled into 45 tankōbon volumes and published by Shogaku-kan from 1970 to 1996. The third type of licensing is *Fashion Licensing*. Versace is an international luxury Italian fashion company that began by serving a female target. As Gianni Versace's popularity increased, so did his brand and the demand for his designs. With the growth of the organization, the brand was able to extend into men's clothing, and not long after, Versace expanded into accessories, jewelry, fragrance, home furnishings, dining and much more. Even though they started out targeting a select market, the opportunity to enter other categories became inevitable. For the brand to grow, the owner chose to extend via licensing, enabling it to develop a powerful connection with consumers. Extending a fashion brand out of its core category into new categories, while also staying true to its expansion point, encourages consumers to consider the brand in other categories (Stankeviciute & Hoffmann, 2010).

The next type of licensing is Technology Licensing (Jiang & Menguc, 2012). For example, major players in the smartphone cover market include Mophie Technology, Moshi, Griffin Technology, Apple, Samsung Electronics, CG Mobile, Incipio, Otter Products and FIT Hon Teng Limited. According to Verified Market Research, the mobile phone protective cases market size was valued at $21.61 billion in 2020 and is projected to reach $35.81 billion by 2028 (Morgan, 2023).

Art Licensing is another type of licensing, which is increasingly growing. Technology is continually changing, and the digital era is becoming more prominent in everyone's lives. Due to technological advancements, more companies can now take advantage of the thousands of pieces of art created by artists each year. These pieces are digitized and made available through Art Licensing to make their brand and products more desirable to consumers (Kerrigan et al., 2011). An example of Art Licensing would be when the Guggenheim Museum showcases thousands of pieces of art in poster form, on mugs, tee shirts and calendars.

An additional type of licensing is music. *Music Licensing* is a bit different from the earlier-mentioned forms of licensing because it consists of three components. The first component is the original score, which is the lyrics, second is the performance of the music, and the third is the overall production. This is a complicated category that is well understood by those in that industry (Klein, 2016). An example of Music Licensing would be with Spotify. They have acquired the rights to broadcast music in digital platforms.

Moving along, the next type of licensing is *Celebrity Licensing*. Beyoncé, over the course of her career has certainly extended herself into the home through her fragrances, apparel, accessories and athletic wear. She is top game, as it relates to celebrities (Cashmore, 2010), and has taken herself from a high position to an even higher position. So, when brand owners or licensees come to her, they know that she is well loved, respected and able to demand a higher royalty rate and a higher performance level overall because of her competence and her fans. Recently the BTS group of Korean pop singers has taken the world by storm. They have licensed their likenesses on dozens of products including apparel, jewelry, photo cards, light sticks, concert gift boxes (to prepare the fan) and even a mystery box full of many exotic items.

Finally, the last type of licensing mentioned is *Sports Licensing*. This type of licensing comprises major sports in the US like baseball, basketball, football, tennis, golf and hockey. All of these sports are exciting to watch, but the world's greatest sport, football, also called soccer in the US, captures the attention of huge brands. The FIFA World Cup was played in Qatar in 2022 and in Australia and New Zealand in 2023. Like the Olympics, FIFA commands a global audience. These sports brands want the opportunity to enable fans to consume them outside of their marquee event (Kwak et al., 2015).

5. Using Media Digital Licensing

Digital licensing refers to just another place to sell licensed products. In this case they are digital products that can either be a representation of something in the physical world or be unique creations in the digital world. Perhaps no greater example of this was when Apple launched iTunes in 2003. It brought music content from all five major labels to sell songs *a la carte* without subscription fees. Within two weeks, iTunes sold 2 million tracks and more than 70 million downloads in its first year (Goldscheider & Gordon, 2006). With the launch of Amazon Music in 2007, Spotify in 2008 and Alexa in 2014, subscription-based streaming music became the norm. Digital licensing has grown exponentially in the last few decades and is expected to continue growing due to the increasing adoption of digital content and services. This market involves the licensing of various types of digital assets, such as software, music, videos, images and other forms of intellectual property. With a shift of the consumers and businesses toward digital consumption, the demand for licensing agreements to access and use these digital assets also increases. Digital Licensing features are based on NFTs (Non-Fungible Tokens), Meta virtual reality devices and Microsoft app AltspaceVR technologies. As pioneers, digital assets in the form of virtual fashions and non-fungible tokens offer consumers a way to shop, exchange goods and inhabit these identities (Borri et al., 2022). According to recent market research (Gherghelas, 2023), spending on NFT acquisitions was estimated to be over $5 billion in 2021. That $5 billion in 2021 will be a significant new addition to the already $300 billion in retail sales of licensed merchandise and services for the global licensing business. Under the licensing business, while a pandemic raged, a brand-new licensed business has taken off, and it is the tip of the digital licensing iceberg. NFTs are not only here to stay but will be a significant part of the coming Metaverse.

The main players are large companies specializing in entertainment, edutainment and video games but also emerging digital content and service providers. The major actors were Disney, but it has disbanded its Next Generation Storytelling and Consumer Experiences

Unit; Meta shut down the Crayta DIY gaming platform that it purchased in 2021. It then launched its Quest Pro mixed reality headset for commercial applications in late 2022 and it will add a consumer version in 2023. Beyond mixed reality, there are more than 200 apps for Meta's virtual reality devices, which have generated more than $1 billion in revenue, according to Zuckerberg (Bobrowsky, 2023). Microsoft's acquisition of social virtual reality app AltspaceVR and proposed purchase of Activision Blizzard in 2023 point to a Metaverse strategy moving forward (Tzanidis & Frew, 2022). Other major players in this space are Sony PlayStation, Epic Games and China's Tencent. Leading brand licensing agency Beanstalk launched Tinderbox in 2013. Tinderbox operates within Beanstalk (Marx, 2013). Beanstalk saw a void in the industry for an agency with expertise in extending digital properties into the consumer products space that could create innovative experiences and products for digital-born properties.

Factors such as the rise of streaming platforms, online gaming, e-learning and the digital transformation of industries contribute to the growth of the digital licensing market. The Metaverse is an immersive virtual world. At the moment it is mainly a commercial enterprise. The building blocks are being rapidly developed by big corporations, including gaming and technology companies. Firms like Facebook, Apple, Google and Microsoft are in direct competition, drawing on their enormous technological resources to design their own Metaverse offerings (Moynihan et al., 2022). With Facebook changing its corporate name to Meta Platforms, Inc., the new focus of the social network/s creates significant opportunities for early adapters seeking participation in the Metaverse. Meta's investment in research toward creating the Metaverse in 2020 was $18 billion and in 2021 is estimated to be an astounding $28 billion. The Metaverse will soon become mainstream, and licensing will play a key role.

From a brand licensing and retail perspective it will be critical to selling products, both digital and physical to consumers. Video Gaming is the marketing tool that all Metaverse providers will initially utilize to capture consumers' attention and engagement (Roettl & Terlutter, 2018). VR technology is increasing with Meta's Oculus Quest Headset, Sony PlayStation Headset and Microsoft HoloLens glasses all competing to be the "Gateway" to the Metaverse. Most importantly for the licensed IP market, game IP will drive the consumer to the Metaverse, increasing the value of gaming companies and demand for consumer products and brand extensions from these games. If the Internet is two-dimensional (text and images on flat screens), the Metaverse is three-dimensional and multi-sensory, including touch. Two of the most popular massive multiplayer game franchises, Fortnite and Roblox, are the most prepared for the Metaverse. Gamers can attend live events, interact with friends' avatars, buy virtual goods and even shop at brand-name stores in these worlds. Several professional sports leagues as well as singers like Elton John and Mariah Carey launched experiences on the Roblox platform, a popular online platform and game creation system that allows users to design, create and play games created by other users. When it comes to virtual products, low prices are not necessarily a guarantee; in 2021, a virtual Gucci handbag listed on Roblox sold for the equivalent of $4,115 (the actual resale price is the virtual currency Roblox); the same handbag, in addition to the real and real-life wearable ones, sells for only $3,400. Because a virtual handbag is not an NFT, it cannot be "used" outside of the Roblox platform. Roblox has also deployed layered clothing that can be added to avatars, a feature that has been adopted by 100–115 million consumers. Gucci is holding a major online exhibition on Roblox, Archetypes Gucci Garden, and recently launched a new GucciTown on Roblox where consumers can have the same experience as in the actual store (Liu, 2022). The platform reported 65 million monthly active users in Q4 2022. Hot Topic, an American retail chain specializing in counterculture-related clothing, accessories and licensed music, partnered with several Roblox designers to launch a collection of Halloween-inspired virtual items in 2022. The range included cosplay hats, die-cut sunglasses, mini-backpacks and other products that served as virtual extensions of IRL (in real-life) items.

Microsoft has been a major force in creating the Metaverse with its Xbox gaming console, HoloLens Virtual Glasses, Teams videoconferencing and its new Mesh service which rolled out in early 2022. Microsoft's acquisition of social virtual reality app AltspaceVR and purchase of Activision Blizzard in 2023 point to a Metaverse strategy moving forward. It appears as if, despite recent cuts, the broader VR ecosystem continues to grow (Chang & Chen, 2017). Other major players in this space are Sony PlayStation, Epic Games and China's Tencent. The pandemic reinforced the creation of virtual worlds. Bloomberg estimates the value of the Metaverse in 2023 to be $800 billion (Boeckem, 2023). The Metaverse brings users into the world where virtual and reality meet, so the brand has to face not only the consumers in the real world, but also the incarnation of the real consumers in the virtual space of the Metaverse, and the brand uses the Metaverse to promote and create momentum, which appropriately meets the social needs of consumers in the virtual space and helps promote the digitalization and rejuvenation of the brand (Liu, 2022).

6. Intellectual Property Rights in the Digital Platforms

The different types of intellectual property include copyrights, trademarks, patents and trade secrets. Each type protects a different aspect of an IP creation (Bouchoux, 2013). Copyright protects original creative works like art, music, literature and software. By default when something is created, it automatically holds copyright protection (Kelly, 2006). Individuals and companies can register their creation with a country's copyright office for added protection. For example, individuals and entities can register their copyright with the US Patent and Trademark Office for protection inside the US. Trademarks protect branding elements such as names, logos and slogans. Trademarks must be registered with relevant authorities to prevent others from using similar branding (Farhana, 2012). Patents protect inventions and processes. Often the process is complex and varies by jurisdiction. To receive protection under patent laws, a technology must fulfill certain criteria, including novelty, inventive step and industrial application (Kash & Kingston, 2001).

Protecting IP in the Metaverse (and other digital platforms) is a crucial consideration as virtual worlds and online environments continue to evolve. The Metaverse is a three-dimensional digital space where businesses, users and organizations can interact with one another. By 2026, 25 percent of people will spend about one hour a day in the Metaverse for entertainment, shopping, education, work, socialization and at least 30 percent of organizations worldwide will have products, such as apparel, automobiles, artwork and other goods in the form of NFTs, available in the Metaverse (Jaimini et al., 2022). As more users enter this space, the question of who owns IP rights to virtual assets and creations becomes increasingly complex. In the Metaverse, Copyright law covers virtual objects like avatars, buildings and landscapes. Trademark law protects logos and other branding materials used within the virtual world, while Patent law applies to technological advancements that arise during the development of the Metaverse (Prajit, 2023).

Aspects worthy of attention to evaluate the use of digital licenses in the Metaverse or in the emerging digital platforms are the following: IP ownership, scope of IP protection, blockchain and interoperability, digital piracy and tools to limit IP infringement.

IP Ownership

There, users can create virtual representations of real-world objects, including copyrighted works or trademarks, that they do not own. Similar to the physical world, builders of the Metaverse should respect the IP rights of designers, inventors and owners of distinctive signs. IP laws protect the intangible elements of an object, whether physical or virtual. Holders of IP rights have the legal right to protect their rights in the Metaverse. When IP rights are infringed upon whether in the physical or Metaverse, owners should prosecute any exploitation of those rights (Prajit, 2023).

Scope of IP Protection

Determining the scope of IP protection in the Metaverse requires careful consideration, as the use of real-world objects in the virtual space may infringe on the IP rights of the real-world owner. There is a need for a clear legal framework that can protect both the rights of the IP owners and the freedom of users to create and interact with virtual objects in the Metaverse. An example of a virtual object that may reside in the Metaverse is an NFT, or non-fungible token. An NFT is a type of digital asset that represents ownership or proof of authenticity using blockchain technology of a unique item or piece of content. Unlike cryptocurrencies such as Bitcoin or Ethereum, which are fungible and can be exchanged on a one-to-one basis, NFTs are indivisible and cannot be exchanged on a like-for-like basis (Prashanth, 2023). While owning an NFT associated with a digital item might indicate ownership of that specific copy of the item, it's important to note that owning an NFT doesn't necessarily grant copyright or exclusive usage rights to the underlying content; it primarily represents ownership of the tokenized version of that content. Storing a protected work in digital form in an electronic medium, such as an NFT or a file displayed in the Metaverse, constitutes a reproduction that requires prior approval from the copyright holder. Therefore, it is crucial to obtain permission from the copyright holder before creating and displaying any virtual assets based on protected works (Rosen, 2022). When the NFT artist Mason Rothschild released a set of "MetaBirkins," including one that reportedly sold for $42,000 in the Metaverse, Hermès, the originator of this bag trademarked as "Birkin" in the real world, filed a complaint in the US Southern District of New York Court. The complaint alleged that the NFT creator was a "digital speculator who is seeking to get rich quick by appropriating the brand METABIRKINS" and that "META-BIRKINS simply rips off Hermès famous BIRKIN trademark by adding the generic prefix 'meta' to the famous trademark BIRKIN." Hermès eventually won its lawsuit when a Manhattan federal jury concluded that the artist's NFTs had violated Hermès' trademark rights, awarding the French fashion house $133,000 in damages (Cooper, 2023).

From the point of view of the digital IP market growth, licensing will play an important role in the Metaverse as brand owners create new IPs as part of their collections and as NFT owners seek to monetize their newly owned NFT IPs. Brand owners can also use NFTs as a launching pad for new products as well, creating a value-add for consumers beyond the physical item. Licensors are exploring licensing activations within virtual worlds that provide an immersive experience, blending digital and physical brand engagement. Because NFTs represent a new and unique form of IP licensing, brand owners have begun mining their archives for digital collectibles. Hollywood Studios like Disney, Warner, Viacom/CBS and NBC/Universal with franchise fan-based IP like Star Trek, Star Wars, Marvel, DC Comics and Harry Potter are creating limited-edition NFTs collectibles as both a revenue driver and a way to engage fans. Sports Leagues too have launched NFT divisions. By far the greatest category of revenue generation has been in fine art, with an NFT by the artist known as Beeple selling for $69 million dollars earlier this year. Just as importantly, NFTs have raised the bar of licensing as a marketing tool. Apart from the rare and valuable ones, many Fast-Moving Consumer Goods (FMCGs) have appropriated NFTs as a pure play marketing tool to appeal to millennials and Gen Z as digital collectibles. McDonalds even created limited-edition McRib NFTs (Ekstract, 2023).

Blockchain and Interoperability

Protecting IP in the Metaverse requires several steps be taken that are foundational such as watermarking or monitoring; however, the key will be to implement as many precautions as possible to make the IP less attractive to would-be pirates. For example, every creation needs to be registered for copyright, trademark or patent protection with the relevant authorities in the jurisdiction of interest. In addition, NFTs use blockchain technology to ensure their ownership is protected. Advancements in technology, such as blockchain-based licensing solutions, can help streamline the licensing process and provide more secure and transparent transactions. This provides the IP owner the ability to take legal action against infringers. A key challenge in the Metaverse is interoperability, which means the existence of a streamlined system so that the end-user experiences a "continuity." The main legal issue with interoperability arises when a company uses its proprietary "coding system" in the Metaverse. Because everything must be shared in order to streamline the "operation," there may be potential issues of IP infringement (Wang et al., 2022).

Digital Piracy

Piracy is likely to flourish in the Metaverse. The digitization of media goods weakened the effective strength of copyright policy by allowing widespread sharing of media files over the Internet, forcing governments to consider how to reform copyright policy to reflect the digital era and forcing firms to consider new strategies in order to compete with online piracy. Digital piracy is estimated by the Global Innovation Policy Center of the US Chamber of Commerce to cost the US economy some $30 billion annually. It is estimated to cost some 70,000 jobs each year (Blackburn et al., 2019). Brand owners could embrace unlimited-term licenses (in-game outfits are kept by players forever), overlapping marketing windows (some brand events are mere days apart or overlap entirely) and little to no editorial control. There are a number of examples of brands' IP rights being violated in the Metaverse. StockX, an online sneaker reseller, has been selling NFT receipts of limited-edition Nikes that include an image of these sneakers. In just one year, relevant brand owners, including Nike, Ralph Lauren, Converse and Walmart, have filed trademarks for a range of virtual goods and services. Companies like

Prada and Gucci are challenging applications filed by unaffiliated individuals attempting to register Prada and Gucci marks in classes for Metaverse-related categories, including downloadable virtual goods, virtual worlds and virtual clothing used in virtual spaces. The number of IP violations in the Metaverse is going to grow. Fashion and consumer goods companies are taking actions to address these violations and to prevent new ones as innovators, brands and pirates alike navigate in the Metaverse. Trade industries have banded together to create a self-regulating organization pending government regulation (Cooper, 2023).

Tools to Limit IP Infringement

To limit IP infringement and improper use in the Metaverse, there are automated tools that search for instances of infringement. If instances of infringement are found, the IP owner could take legal action to protect their rights. Moreover, the contract clauses to place particularly sensitive or proprietary materials in the Metaverse can be added, together with clear lines about the ownership of content that can be posted in virtual worlds as in the real world. This step provides IP owners with additional income streams while helping to ensure that their IP is used in a manner consistent with their wishes. Another tool to limit IP infringement is to define the terms of use for digital creations. Like traditional licensing agreements, specific direction can be stipulated on how the IP can be used, shared or modified in the Metaverse (Cutler & Spinelli, 2022). Additional steps to protect IP in the Metaverse include:

- Watermarking and Digital Signatures: For visual content like images or videos, watermarking provides a clear way to assert ownership. Additionally, using digital signatures can prove authenticity of ownership.
- Blockchain Technology: Some platforms are exploring the use of blockchain to establish ownership and provenance of digital assets. This technology can enhance transparency and trust in the Metaverse.
- Digital Rights Management (DRM): DRM solutions offer IP owners the ability to control and manage how their digital content, how it is accessed, used and distributed. DRM can restrict unauthorized copying and sharing.
- EULA and Terms of Service: End-User License Agreements (EULAs) and Terms of Service (ToS) state the rules and restrictions for using digital content within virtual worlds and online platforms. A ToS agreement provides a legal recourse if those conditions are violated.
- Monitor and Enforce: Monitoring the Metaverse and digital platforms for unauthorized use of IP allows owners to take appropriate actions against infringers, which may include sending cease and desist notices to offenders or pursuing legal action when necessary.
- Collaboration Agreements: These serve to protect IP owners when collaborating with entities in the Metaverse, specifically with respect to ownership, usage and distribution of jointly created content.
- Continuous Education: Laws and regulations related to IP in the Metaverse are still evolving. IP owners should stay updated with legal developments and consult with legal professionals who specialize in IP and technology law.

In conclusion, the Metaverse is a unique and rapidly evolving space. Protecting IP requires a combination of traditional legal strategies and innovative technological solutions.

Case #1 – Using Media Digital Licensing – Crayola Partners with TheSoul Publishing to Amplify Digital Influence

Crayola Case Study – Crayola Partners with TheSoul Publishing to Amplify Digital Influence

Licensor: Crayola, www.crayola.com. Founded in 1885 in Easton -Pennsylvania under the name of Binney & Smith, Crayola is the global leader of creative expression products. The company has a broad portfolio of innovative brands and products, which include wide ranges of colors and artistic tools, toys and creative activities for edutainment.

Licensee: TheSoul Publishing, www.thesoul-publishing.com. This company is the world's leading digital studio that produces engaging, positive and original content for a global audience. TheSoul Publishing showcases entertaining brands in 21 different languages, which are distributed through a social media-driven cross-platform network. With more than 1.5 billion social media followers across Facebook, Instagram, TikTok, YouTube, Pinterest and Snapchat, TheSoul Publishing creates content for all ages. Current initiatives include expansion across additional social media, music, podcast and streaming platforms.

Geographic Area: Worldwide

Date: June 2023

FIGURE 1.1   Crayola TheSoul Publishing Composite Logo

Source: Credit: Craig Radow, TheSoul Publishing

Situation. TheSoul Publishing, an award-winning digital content creation studio, and Crayola, the global leader of creative expression products, saw the opportunity to expand their partnership building on the success they saw on Crayola's YouTube channel performance. Crayola entered a licensing agreement in Q1 2023 with TheSoul Publishing for co-produced digital content on Crayola-owned social media channels.

Task. Grow Crayola's content library with programming that sparks creative self-expression in every child. Broaden Crayola's digital reach and influence, ensuring more audiences can engage with the company's creative content.

Action. Partner with TheSoul Publishing based on its global reach and track record of creating high-quality video content and growing brands on social media to include management of YouTube TikTok and Pinterest.

Results. From Q4 2022 compared to Q2 2023, total watch hours surged, increasing by 30×. Organic views by 40×. The number of published videos increased significantly, 6× more videos per month. The partnership fueled an increase in new subscribers to Crayola's YouTube channel. These results demonstrate the effectiveness of Crayola and TheSoul's partnership in boosting digital engagement and expanding the brand's reach across social media.

Noteworthy. Victoria Lozano, Executive Vice President, Marketing at Crayola, said, "The extraordinary growth we have achieved together validates this partnership, and we are eager to explore the new heights we can reach in the next phase of this journey." Patrik Wilkens, Vice President of Operations at TheSoul Publishing, said,

The remarkable growth we've seen in views and watch hours truly underscores the power of our partnership. We're even more thrilled about the surge in new subscribers. This tells us that the content isn't just being watched, it's being eagerly anticipated and regularly consumed by a dedicated and growing fan base.

FIGURE 1.2   TheSoul Publishing – Crayola

Source: Credit: Craig Radow, TheSoul Publishing

Case #2 – Using Media Digital Licensing – Kartoon Studios Partners with VeVe for Stan Lee Digital Collectibles

Kartoon Studios Case Study – Kartoon Studios Partners with VeVe for Stan Lee Digital Collectibles

Licensor: Kartoon Studios, www.kartoonstudios.com. Through a joint venture with POW! Entertainment, Kartoon Studios owns and manages the global rights to the legendary Stan Lee's name, physical likeness, voice, signature and IP, called Stan Lee Universe.

Licensee: VeVe Digital Collectibles. VeVe is a mobile application available for Android and iOS devices, developed by Ecomi. The app serves as a platform for the buying and selling of licensed digital collectibles, utilizing non-fungible token technology.

Licensed Property: Stan Lee. Stanley Martin Lieber (1922–2018), aka Stan Lee, is a famous cartoonist, editor, film and television producer.

Geographical Area: Worldwide

Date: July, 2023

Situation: Renowned artist Stan Lee worked in the comic book business for almost 80 years, revolutionizing the industry and co-creating some famous characters. "Nuff Said" was one of his famous signature expressions.

Task: Develop four digital collectibles of Stan Lee for fans in Chibi style, a caricature originating in Japan and common in anime and manga where characters are drawn in an exaggerated way, typically small and chubby with stubby limbs, oversized heads and minimal detail. Timing to commemorate Stan Lee's 100th year.

Action: Sign Veve Digital to create a collection that includes: The King of Cameos, Nuff Said!, Excelsior! ("ever upward") and The Amazing Stan Lee.

Results: Collection sold through shortly after launch on July 18. The total drop of over 8,000 digital collectibles sold out immediately. This followed a successful opening of the Stan Lee Exhibit at The Comic-Con Museum in San Diego, California.

Noteworthy: Lloyd Mintz, SVP, Global Consumer Products, Kartoon Studios, stated: "We are thrilled with the results of this first venture in digital collectibles. That there was a complete sell through, and the fact that it was nearly instantaneous is a very strong indicator of the extraordinary passion that fans have for Stan Lee." David Yu, CEO, VeVe Digital Collectibles commented: "This sale marks an important turning point in the digital collectibles market."

Case #3 – The Licensing Program between Bored of Directors and Bioworld Merchandising

Licensor: NFIP Holdings d/b/a Bored of Directors, NFIP is an NFT IP holding company which specializes in monetizing NFT value through collective asset pooling and conversion into consumer goods, services and partnerships.

Founder: Alex Locke, Esq

Master Apparel Licensee: Bioworld Merchandising + Multiple Other Licenses Secured

Licensing Agency: Brand Central

Licensed Property: 11 Bored Ape Yacht Club NFTs

NFT Owners: 10 separate individuals

Geographic Area: North America, Europe, Malaysia, South America, UK, South Africa and South Korea

Date: May 2022

Situation: Alex Locke, founder of Bored of Directors, understood the latent value in the 11 Bored Ape Yacht Club NFTs given the growth of the Metaverse. NFIP Holdings mission is to bring the excitement of Web3, NFTs and the Metaverse to the world through licensed products. NFIP Holdings has been involved in NFTs since its infancy. Brand Central LLC is a premier global brand consultancy that provides comprehensive business solutions in the areas of brand extensions, trend intelligence and manufacturer representation to some of the world's most recognized brands, including Mars Wrigley, Black Paper Party and Mister Rogers Neighborhood.

FIGURE 1.3   Bored of Directors Brand
Source: Credit: Alex Locke, Bored of Directors

Task: NFIP Holdings knew that if they could convince ten independent owners of Bored Ape Yacht Club NFTs of the potential they could create a significant opportunity to break ground in the area of licensing NFTs in the Metaverse which had yet to tap into the physical world, and form the brand Bored of Directors. Locke understood that he would need to create derivative artwork and assets for each BAYC NFT and through the help of Brand Central, create a full style guide featuring on trend images, personalities and graphics and the collective plans to position the program for success and bring more Bored Ape owners on board as the brand grew, which was important to maintain freshness. Once this was in place, the Bored of Directors would need to find licensees for each of the major categories that were willing to support the program. The biggest would be for apparel.

Action: According to Licensing International, Brand Central, the exclusive global licensing agency for Bored of Directors and their network of leading global subagents closed multiple licensing partners around the globe by October 2022 in the US, UK, Europe, Mexico, South Korea and Israel. A portion has been with Bioworld as their master apparel licensee. For over 20 years Bioworld has partnered with the biggest brands in the world. They have over 20 product categories and complete retail distribution in all tiers including Amazon and direct-to-consumer. Moreover, they line up retail partnerships to assist in the distribution. In the US, this included the following licensees (categories of merchandise):

- Bioworld (Apparel, Headwear, Bags and Impulse Items)
- Brand Collective (Headwear, Cold Weather Accessories, Bags, Wallets/Wristlets, Luggage & Luggage Accessories)
- Concept One (Headwear, Cold Weather Accessories, Bags, Wallets/Wristlets, Luggage & Luggage Accessories)

- Just Funky (Beverageware, Blankets/Throws, Plush, Bag Clips, Acrylic Stands, Tableware/Dishware, Journals/Notebooks, Pens/Pen Toppers, Cable Covers, Umbrellas, Wall Art, Sunshades, License Plate Frames, Snow Globes, Air Fresheners)
- Prime 3D (Puzzles)
- Textiss (Headwear, Socks)

Results: Bored of Directors' Bored Ape Yacht Club NFTs are regarded as a gold standard for the business. With a network of 11 global agents, headed by Brand Central, the program has landed more than 50 licensing deals across a range of categories including apparel, toys and games, and food and beverage with over 450 SKUs in development. As of the second quarter of 2023, the product is distributed in 15 countries. Current retailers include Kohls (US), Pac Sun (US), Walmart (US), Target (US), FashionNova (US), Amazon (US, UK, Europe), Index/Ripley (Peru), C&A (Germany), Lindex (Sweden, Norway, Finland, Denmark), Celio (France), AW LAB (Italy), Hybris (Sweden, Denmark, Norway, Finland, Poland), Funky Buddha (Greece, Cyprus), Suburbia (Mexico), and Target Australia (Australia). Distribution is expected in 361 (China), The Works (UK), B&W (UK) and Dapper Stores (Malaysia) by 2024. And for Bored of Directors, a collective of 10 NFT owners, it has been a business that commands six figures in minimum guarantees and over $1 million in the aggregate and 10–15 percent royalty rates on two to four year contracts as apparel licensees gain distribution through Walmart, Target and other retailers. The Bored of Directors brand was nominated by Licensing International for a global Licensing Excellence award for Best Brands of 2022 for the Digitally Native, Gaming and NFT category.

Noteworthy: As consumers' relationships with NFTs evolve, many in the industry – including Bored of Directors – are transitioning to a more design-driven business that extends well beyond the investment value of the token itself. Bored Ape has 11 different characters.

FIGURE 1.4 Bored of Directors Bag Clip

Source: Credit: Alex Locke, Bored of Directors

"It is the design that has the market value and that, as a piece of art, allows you to go into licensing," said Rob Corney, Group Managing Director at Bulldog Licensing, which represents the Bored of Directors in the UK. "When there is a new media, we should think about what the currency is and what is being bought and sold. If it has brand equity and integrity as a concept, then it's made for licensing" (Seavy, 2023).

FIGURE 1.5   Bored of Directors Buildable Figurine

Source: Credit: Alex Locke, Bored of Directors

FIGURE 1.6   Bored of Directors Tee Shirts

Source: Credit: Alex Locke, Bored of Directors

FIGURE 1.7 Bored of Directors 361 ball sneaker ad

Source: Credit: Alex Locke, Bored of Directors

FIGURE 1.8 Bored of Directors apparel

Source: Credit: Alex Locke, Bored of Directors

WHAT ALEX LOCKE THINKS ABOUT DIGITAL PLATFORMS

In this interview of December 1, 2022, Pete Canalichio, brand strategist and licensing expert, discussed with Alex Locke, Esq., attorney, entrepreneur and licensing and NFT expert, about how to manage licensing in the digital world. The interview took place over Zoom with Pete located in his office in Atlanta and Alex in his office located in New York City. The interview lasted approximately one hour. Here, an excerpt of the interview is reported (Table 1.4). The central topic is about the value of the NFT in making the Bored Apes Yacht Club program different and special.

TABLE 1.4 Digital Licensings in the Opinion of an Expert

Topic	Answers
The Bored Ape Yacht Club concept	An NFT is a digital representation of ownership. Where it gets tricky is that sometimes the two are one and the same. That would be the Bored Ape example where the token is also the art, or the asset. The NFT could have no image. It's like a digital deed to a house. If it's a physical house, then it's just the digital deed in that example. Theoretically let's say it's a house that's going to live in a Metaverse. It could be both at the same time. You could have a digital NFT that represents the physical property and represents the digital property. It could be the digital receipt. Regardless of the tech and medium, I knew that, at its core, this was a character-driven property, which always needs representation in the mainstream both through content and consumer goods to stay relevant and generate revenue.
	There appears to be a resistance among the Web3.0 world as it is related to making their brands more accessible to mainstream society or "off-chain" if you will. To me this is a bit reminiscent of the early days of Hip-Hop where the artists' goal was to sell records and get their name out there but viewed distributing on the radio as selling out. As it turns out, making your art available for the masses is the only way to achieve their goals and Hip-Hop being played on the radio was inevitable. That is what I see with Web3.0 and NFTs. In this analogy, the radio is the sale of consumer goods via traditional channels.
A digital representation of ownership	A digital receipt is like the Rolex analogy. If you buy a Rolex, it comes with a card that has your serial number. The [serial number is] unique to that Rolex. If it gets stolen and you report it to the police, you are protected if someone tries to sell it. The serial number is your proof of a one-of-one ownership of something.
	NFT, that digital representation, manifests itself in some kind of image. Or it could be a solid white square and that digital code is representing a solid white square which you can't really see the edges of on a white screen. You have a digital wallet that shows the NFTs you own.

(Continued)

TABLE 1.4 (Continued)

Topic	Answers
Proof of digital ownership to track what people own	If everyone going forward starts using NFTs as proof of ownership rather than traditional methods, on your phone you could verify and prove, and have an index, of every asset you own in a little file. It could exist in an app or on a web browser or at some point on somebody's iris. Based on this, we could verify someone owns x, y and z digital or physical assets.
The promise of decentralization	At its core the promise of Web3.0, blockchain, means that everything is not centralized in one location, on one server. There are bits and pieces of code and elements moving around all the time. If someone came into my office right now and unplugged the entire server room, everything is gone. With blockchain those bits are moving across nodes across the world and not static. Parts of it always sit all over the place. So that's decentralization.
	If all my money is in a centralized bank, I call Chase, that's a central location for me to call. The money is decentralized. There's a benefit of it not being in one spot. If that place gets hacked, it's over. To get business done a lot of times you need the central authority decision-maker to act. So, there's a large promise of this Web3.0 and the decentralization. It is democratization and power to the people and things of that nature, which is great in theory, but you know for licensing what are you going to do? Every NFT owner in the world can find them through anonymous ledgers and code. That's the insanity of it because they don't want to be known. They are willing to be known only under certain circumstances. So, it just makes it difficult.
	If I'm a brand owner or I'm a retailer what they're debating now is which Metaverse do I want my presence to be. So, is it going to be Facebook's iteration or is it going to be some other entity? The fact that there are so many competing Metaverse is somewhat counter-intuitive to the whole purpose of it anyway. Do we think they'll consolidate at some point?
	I think there's probably going to have to be some consolidation. If I'm a brand owner, why wouldn't I just build my own experience?
The Metaverse as a recreation of the physical world	I always saw the dream and promise of virtual reality as an escape where there's a crazy game or experience that I would never have in real life. I never thought the first use case is going to be recreating the real world. Why the hell do I want to go into that? I think it was silly to brand this whole thing as Web3.0 and the Metaverse and make it sound so intangible. It's just an evolution in what's already been happening, digital licensing that's been happening for 20 years.

Topic	Answers
The goal of Metaverse competitors	Competitors in the Metaverse want to keep you on their platform as long as possible. The incentive for the consumer is you can only get a particular product within their Metaverse. That's the specialness of this opportunity. It compels these platforms to fight tooth and nail not to agree to be collaborative because then when a consumer goes into their world it's no different. It's not more special.
e-Commerce differs in the Metaverse	The NFT sale cuts out the middleman. Apple currently takes a 30 percent commission on purchases made in the Apple App Store. With NFTs, there is no App Store; it's a direct-to-direct transaction. It's beneficial for the consumer. The Metas of the world are going to get their money. They haven't figured out how they're going to do it. Everyone's mission statement is altruism but they're not doing this for nothing.
Valuing an NFT	I attended a legal seminar about valuing art. I was excited to finally get some formula. Instead, they told me the value of the art is the price that the painter is comfortable parting with their creation. Alternatively, the value is what somebody's willing to pay based on the joy it brings to them. It's kind of the same way with the NFTs. The benefit is being in an exclusive club. It could be worth a lot of money to somebody. NFT owners are buying access. There are a million different business models and things that the NFT can represent. The NFT is the vehicle. It's not the end product. The creativity doesn't end when the NFT is created. That's when it starts. It's a seamless way for someone to engage and have a direct line with the consumer. The industry needs to come up with creative ways to deliver the promise. The NFT gets the owner special access that other people don't have. It's the value of what the creator gives that will impact how compelling it becomes.
The uniqueness of owning an NFT	In the case of the Bored Apes Yacht Club, the first thing that was given was the right for the owner to commercialize the artwork. Disney's never going to give an NFT for Mickey Mouse. Instead of someone buying a lifetime Fastpass at Disney World, a Mickey Mouse NFT could get someone access at all the parks. They could cut the line, get more face time with the Disney Princesses, or a cameo with Iron Man. With 3D printing, maybe someone could get a custom Marvel superhero action figure. Disney could access its archival footage of unreleased scenes that are collecting dust. Someone could use an NFT to get access to a movie that was never released or a director's cut that never went public, or bloopers, or deleted scenes. It's about making unique offerings and giving value. I think everyone has gotten so focused on the [Metaverse] and its craziness. We'll be one of the pioneers in this space and we'll be remembered and revered for that.

(Continued)

TABLE 1.4 (Continued)

Topic	Answers
How licensors will utilize NFTs in the Metaverse	When someone purchases an NFT they do not own the trademark or original piece of art. Instead, when someone owns the NFT token, they also get benefits that come with it. Let's say a new Black Panther movie is coming out. In this example, everyone who owns a specific promotional Black Panther movie NFT would get access to watch the premiere a week early at a specific location. This is the type of thing that could occur. You cannot buy a ticket to the premiere for early access; you have to own the Black Panther NFT. You're the SuperFan who has the NFT which puts you in the private group chat with all the other NFT owners that also all have the same affinity for the same cause. You're all promoting it to each other and talking about it because you're all on the same page. That's why you own the NFT. Only people who own that NFT, which is a one-to-one relationship, get access to whatever specific ownership brings. Some Licensors are simply taking existing imagery and converting it into NFTs. It is important to note that the NFT is not the product; it is the medium. Simply converting your existing property into NFT format and passing it off as a new product is a bad idea in my opinion. That would be akin to re-mastering a VHS as a DVD and calling it a new movie. It is not a new movie; it is the same movie delivered via a new medium.
Increasing the value of NFTs in the Metaverse?	The Bored Ape Yacht Club has new concerts and music festivals and there are no tickets for sale. There's no guest list. Your NFT is your pass to get into the venue. Either you have it or you don't. If I owned a stadium or a sports team, I'd sell the digital component to a season ticket from a VR perspective. It's like sitting courtside. The NFT could be your digital courtside season ticket. Perhaps there's a special camera that's at the baseline that gives you a camera angle that nobody else has. That's unique to that exact vantage point. The possibilities are infinite. The creativity of the individual will drive what's possible. We are trying to create a stronger affinity. Alternatively, we can just try to make some money with the NFT. In that case, the NFT could be more product-driven. You, as the owner of the NFT, get early access to the product. You get some discounts on exclusive products for more money, prestige products. That's your ticket to the event. Think about Vegas as an analogy. It's cheap to stay in Vegas because once you're there you spend a lot of money. So, this [NFT] can get you in there and then you still have to buy "concessions."

References

Bass, A. (2004). Licensed extensions – stretching to communicate. *Journal of Brand Management*, *12*(1), 31–38.

Batra, R., Lenk, P., & Wedel, M. (2010). Brand extension strategy planning: Empirical estimation of brand – category personality fit and atypicality. *Journal of Marketing Research*, *47*(2), 335–347.

Blackburn, D., Eisenach, J., & Harrison Jr., D. (2019). *Impacts of digital video piracy on the U.S. economy*. Global Innovation Policy Center, U.S. Chamber of Commerce.

Bobrowsky, M. (2023). TikTok's parent takes on meta in battle for virtual-reality market. *Wall Street Journal*. www.wsj.com/articles/tiktoks-parent-takes-on-meta-in-battle-for-virtual-reality-market-dd4abdb6

Boeckem, B. (2023). Where the metaverse makes a difference. *Forbes*. www.forbes.com/sites/forbestechcouncil/2023/06/07/where-the-metaverse-makes-a-difference/?sh=70430b4313e8

Borri, N., Liu, Y., & Tsyvinski, A. (2022). *The economics of non-Fungible tokens*. http://dx.doi.org/10.2139/ssrn.4052045

Bouchoux, D. E. (2013). *Intellectual property: The law of trademarks, copyrights, patents, and trade secrets*. Delmar, Cengage Learning.

Brody, A. L., & Lord, J. B. (Eds.). (2007). *Developing new food products for a changing marketplace*. CRC Press.

Canalichio, P. (2018). *Expand, grow, thrive: 5 Proven steps to turn good brands into global brands through the LASSO method*. Emerald Publishing Limited.

Cashmore, E. (2010). Buying Beyoncé. *Celebrity Studies*, *1*(2), 135–150.

Chang, S. N., & Chen, W. L. (2017, May). Does visualize industries matter? A technology foresight of global virtual reality and augmented reality industry. In *2017 International Conference on Applied System Innovation (ICASI)* (pp. 382–385). IEEE.

Chevalier, M., & Mazzalovo, G. (2008). *Luxury brand management: A world of privilege*. John Wiley & Sons.

Colucci, M., Montaguti, E., & Lago, U. (2008). Managing brand extension via licensing: An investigation into the high-end fashion industry. *International Journal of Research in Marketing*, *25*(2), 129–137.

Cooper, J. (2023). *Intellectual property piracy in the time of the metaverse*. The Law Review of the Franklin Pierce Center for IP. https://law.unh.edu/blog/2023/06/idea-volume-63-number-3

Cowen, T., & Crampton, E. (2002). *Market failure or success*. Edward Elgar.

Crombar, B. (2023). *2,000 Disney characters names list (A-Z)*. Featured Animation.

Cutler, M., & Spinelli, M. (2022). *Intellectual property in the metaverse and the challenges of regulating a lawless frontier*. Harness IP. https://www2.deloitte.com/us/en/pages/consumer-business/articles/retail-distribution-industry-outlook.html

Ekstract, S. (2023). *Extracts from Ekstract: What's in store for 2023?* Licensing International.

Farhana, M. (2012). Brand elements lead to brand equity: Differentiate or die. *Information Management and Business Review*, *4*(4), 223–233.

Gherghelas, S. (2023). *NFT marketplace war doubles trading volume in first quarter*. DappRadar.

Goldscheider, R., & Gordon, A. H. (Eds.). (2006). *Licensing best practices: Strategic, territorial, and technology issues*. John Wiley & Sons.

Haigh, D., & Knowles, J. (2004). Don't waste time with brand valuation. *Marketing NPV*, 5.

Hosany, S., Prayag, G., Martin, D., & Lee, W. Y. (2013). Theory and strategies of anthropomorphic brand characters from Peter Rabbit, Mickey Mouse, and Ronald McDonald, to Hello Kitty. *Journal of Marketing Management*, *29*(1–2), 48–68.

Jaimini, U., Zhang, T., Brikis, G. O., & Sheth, A. (2022). iMetaverseKG: Industrial metaverse knowledge graph to promote interoperability in design and engineering applications. *IEEE Internet Computing*, *26*(6), 59–67.

Jayachandran, S., Kaufman, P., Kumar, V., & Hewett, K. (2013). Brand licensing: What drives royalty rates? *Journal of Marketing*, *77*(5), 108–122.

Jiang, M. S., & Menguc, B. (2012). Brand as credible commitment in embedded licensing: A transaction cost perspective. *International Marketing Review*, *29*(2), 134–150.

Kash, D. E., & Kingston, W. (2001). Patents in a world of complex technologies. *Science and Public Policy*, *28*(1), 11–22.

Kelly, K. (2006). Scan this book! *The New York Times*, p. 14.

Kerrigan, F., Brownlie, D., Hewer, P., & Daza-LeTouze, C. (2011). 'Spinning' Warhol: Celebrity brand theoretics and the logic of the celebrity brand. *Journal of Marketing Management*, *27*(13–14), 1504–1524.

Klein, B. (2016). *As heard on TV: Popular music in advertising*. Routledge.

Kwak, D. H., Kwon, Y., & Lim, C. (2015). Licensing a sports brand: Effects of team brand cue, identification, and performance priming on multidimensional values and purchase intentions. *Journal of Product & Brand Management*, *24*(3), 198–210.

Laforet, S., & Saunders, J. (2005). Managing brand portfolios: How strategies have changed. *Journal of Advertising Research*, *45*(3), 314–327.

Liu, J. (2022). *Metaverse and brand: A study of luxury brand digital marketing strategy – taking Gucci as an example*. School of Art & Science, Indiana University at Bloomington.

Martensen, K. (2003). How much for the brand license? Valuation of brand extension license opportunities, elektronisch veröffentlich unter der URL http://www. goldmarks. net/pdf/how_much_for_the_brand_license. pdf, abgerufen am, 6, 2011.

Marx, L. (2013). Beanstalk launches new digital licensing division, tinderbox. *PR Newswire*. www.prnewswire.com/news-releases/beanstalk-launches-new-digital-licensing-division-tinderbox-211179461.html

Meschnig, A., Decker-Lange, C., & Dubiel, A. (2023). Burning the candle at both ends: How to balance potential profitability and brand protection when licensing brands. *European Journal of Marketing*. https://kclpure.kcl.ac.uk/portal/en/publications/burning-the-candle-at-bothends-how-to-balance-potential-profitab

Michel, G., & Donthu, N. (2014). Why negative brand extension evaluations do not always negatively affect the brand: The role of central and peripheral brand associations. *Journal of Business Research*, *67*(12), 2611–2619.

Morgan, M. (2023). *Smartphone accessories licensing*. License Global.

Moynihan, H., Buchser, M., & Wallace, J. (2022). *What is the metaverse? Explaining what is meant by the metaverse, how the metaverse will be accessed, and why it requires ambitious, agile regulation*. Chatham House.

Nimmer, R. T., & Dodd, J. C. (2005). *Modern licensing law*. Thomson West.

Prajit, G. (2023). Protecting intellectual property in the metaverse: Challenges, opportunities, and recent case laws. *The Times of India*. https://timesofindia.indiatimes.com/blogs/voices/protecting-intellectual-property-in-the-metaverse-challenges-opportunities-and-recent-case-laws/

Prashanth, D. (2023). *Unlocking the world of NFTs: Beyond apes and punks*. Nasdaq.

Progoff, S., & Palladino, V. N. (2005). Tips for successful trademark licensing. *Intellectual Asset Management*, *19*.

Roettl, J., & Terlutter, R. (2018). The same video game in 2D, 3D or virtual reality – how does technology impact game evaluation and brand placements? *PLoS One*, *13*(7), e0200724.

Rosen, A. (2022). *What does NFT mean? A guide to non-fungible tokens*. NerdWallet.

Rotfeld, H. J. (2008). Brand image of company names matters in ways that can't be ignored. *Journal of Product & Brand Management*, *17*(2), 121–122.

Santo, A. (2015). *Selling the silver bullet: The lone ranger and transmedia brand licensing*. University of Texas Press.

Seavy, M. (2023). *Flavors from the bar to the grill: Fireball™, Buffalo Trace™ and Southern Comfort™- inspired seasonings set to launch this month*. Licensing international.

Sherman, A. (2011). *Franchising and licensing: Two powerful ways to grow your business in any economy*. Amacom/Harper Collins.

Stankeviciute, R., & Hoffmann, J. (2010). The impact of brand extension on the parent luxury fashion brand: The cases of Giorgio Armani, Calvin Klein and Jimmy Choo. *Journal of Global Fashion Marketing*, *1*(2), 119–128.

Stone, M., & Trebbien, J. D. (2019). Brand licensing: A powerful marketing tool for today's shopping battlefield. *Journal of Brand Strategy*, *8*(3), 207–217.

Tzanidis, T., & Frew, M. (2022). How Microsoft's Activision blizzard takeover will drive metaverse gaming into the mass market. *The Conversation*. https://theconversation.com/how-microsofts-activision-blizzard-takeover-will-drive-metaverse-gaming-into-the-mass-market-175453

Wang, Y., Su, Z., Zhang, N., Xing, R., Liu, D., Luan, T. H., & Shen, X. (2022). A survey on metaverse: Fundamentals, security, and privacy. *IEEE Communications Surveys & Tutorials*, *25*(1), 319–352.

Wiedmann, K. P., & Ludewig, D. (2008). How risky are brand licensing strategies in view of customer perceptions and reactions? *Journal of General Management*, *33*(3), 31–52.

2

CHARTING THE PATH FOR ENDURING BRAND LICENSING PROGRAMS

Learning Objectives

The aim of the chapter is to provide content and tools to answer the following questions: Are you qualified to be a licensee or a licensor? Are you able to fill the shoes of your counterpart? How do you build an effective licensing program? After reading this chapter, readers will be able to understand why brand owners choose to license their brand and why manufacturers and retailers license-in brands. Readers will learn about the main ways to license a brand and the roles involved in the licensing process. They will be able to identify the flow of how products are created and the flow of royalty payments as essential parts of the brand licensing relationship. Finally, they will be able to evaluate and compare the benefits that make licensing so attractive to brand owners and manufacturers alike and to break down the brand licensing process into steps so as to identify areas of value for building an effective and enduring brand licensing program.

Keywords: Licensing-out, Licensing-in, Cross-licensing, Role Players, Licensed Product Flow, Royalty Payments Flow, Brand Licensing Program in Steps.

1. Current State of Licensing

Brand licenses are distinctive assets whose value lies in the reputation, image, quality and stylistic standards associated with the brand. They have the task of brand orientation, highlighting the functional and emotional components that characterize the brand positioning statement (Cross, 2015). As such, branding assets are protected by intellectual property, trademark and patent rights, whose value orientates the amount of royalties (Jayachandran et al., 2013). The protection concerns the image and reputation of the original brand as well as compliance with the design and quality standards of the licensed products in line with what is established by the licensor company. The valuable brand can be used as a strategic lever to successfully compete in the markets, but building its success requires strategic planning and investments (Aloosh et al., 2006). Key components of branding strategies are

DOI: 10.4324/9781003364566-3

brand equity, building strong brands, brand positioning and managing brands (Muhonen et al., 2017). Brand licensing allows early-stage licensees to acquire external knowledge to access new markets, get to know suppliers and other supply chain entities even in the absence of relationships, and have a portfolio of internationally known brands despite not having adequate marketing skills to operate in foreign or global markets. Brand licensing can be a valid tool also for licensees already present on the market, to consolidate their position in new market segments and to diversify their own product offer.

Previous studies (Sherman, 1991, Reese, 2011; Perrier, 1998; Simon & Battersby, 2011) provided a complete overview of how to structure and run a licensing program, whether focused on brands, entertainment, fashion, sports, celebrities or nonprofit properties. Others (Goldscheider, 2002) offered real-world analyses of trends and procedures, as well as a look into the future of licensing and the identification of opportunities to be found there. Other authors (Robinson et al., 2015; Travaglini et al., 2015; Stone, 2018) analyzed the value created for a licensor and how to evaluate and maximize opportunities for well-known brands to capitalize on their equity. They examined the brand development strategy model through licensing and looked at new and emerging ways licensing can be used to achieve specific brand objectives. Royalty rates were analyzed across industries offering guidelines that would help ensure licensing agreements persisted from a financial perspective (Parr, 2007). Licensing offers new entry points for people to discover a brand (Lotman, 2020). Through licensing, brands can outflank the competition by entering unexplored categories and connecting with new customers. Studies (Robinson et al., 2015) showed that brand extension and expansion are effective growth strategies for leveraging the brand value in other product lines or product categories. To this end, particular attention has been given to the business, marketing and branding aspects of licenses (Stone, 2018). Lotman (2020) developed a step-by-step process that enables brands not only to expand into new categories but also to deepen relationships with existing customers. The long-lasting licensing management (Canalichio, 2018) considers the entire licensing process and focuses on those concepts that make licensing partnerships enduring, profitable and successful. Brand resources are valuable components both for the licensor and the licensee.

Brand licensing strategies are part of the most recent debate following the digital platforms diffusion. In virtual and augmented reality environments, including the Metaverse, digital licenses find opportunities and room for growth but are also exposed to the risks of intellectual property piracy (Prajit, 2023; Cooper, 2023).

Brand licensing is also a strategic choice for small- and medium-sized enterprises (Cardinali et al., 2019) to enhance brand orientation and brand capabilities. Traditionally, SMEs face growth independently, investing in innovation and in the internationalization of their brand, leveraging internal resources or through collaboration agreements and strategic alliances. Less attention is given to growth through brand licensing, that is, long-lasting partnerships that aim to exploit the value of the brand with win-win strategies for both the brand owner and the licensee. Some studies (Odoom et al., 2017) suggest that the answer to the SMEs development and growth can be found in brand licensing. Creating brand value (Petromilli et al., 2002) requires a long-term investment, with a brand positioning, brand name and brand development in line with the company's values and a distinctive set of resources and skills (Aloosh et al., 2006). Investments in building brand equity as well as budget and time constraints make brand licensing an accessible strategic option. It allows companies, especially small- and medium-sized ones, to overcome the barriers associated with brand development and to grow more rapidly in the markets. SMEs can enhance their manufacturing and distribution opportunities with well-known brands and acquire external capabilities. In summary, brand licensing can represent an opportunity for SMEs. First, they may have externally sourced branding assets, such as licenses, trademarks and patents, to acquire strategic and exclusive property rights. Second, they can develop the market knowledge and the relational skills of the licensors, to expand into different markets or geographical areas. Table 2.1 summarizes the above-mentioned brand licensing studies.

TABLE 2.1 Overview of Brand Licensing Studies

Author	Title	Year	Publisher
Aloosh, A., Aloosh, M., Tarighati, T., & Baghini, H. S.	Extended products branding issues	2006	IEEE International Technology Management Conference
Batra, R., Lenk, P. and Wedel, M.	Brand extension strategy planning: Empirical estimation of brand – category personality fit and atypicality	2010	Journal of marketing research, 47(2), pp. 335–347
Canalichio, Pete	Expand, Grow, Thrive: 5 Proven Steps To Turn Good Brands Into Global Brands Through The LASSO Method	2018	Emerald
Cardinali, S., Travaglini, M. and Giovannetti, M.	Increasing Brand Orientation and Brand Capabilities Using Licensing: an Opportunity for SMEs in International Markets	2019	Journal of the Knowledge Economy, 10(4), pp. 1808–1830
Cooper, J.	Intellectual Property Piracy in the Time of the Metaverse	2023	IDEA, 63
Cross, B.	The effective use of licensing in brand strategy	2015	Journal of Brand Strategy, 4(4), pp. 357–362
Goldscheider, R. and Gordon, A.	Licensing Best Practices: Strategic, Territorial and Technology Issues	2006	John Wiley & Sons
Jayachandran, S., Kaufman, P., Kumar, V. and Hewett, K.	Brand licensing: What drives royalty rates?	2013	Journal of Marketing, 77(5), pp. 108–122
Odoom, R., Agbemabiese, G. C., Anning-Dorson, T., & Mensah, P.	Branding capabilities and SME performance in an emerging market: The moderating effect of brand regulations	2017	Marketing Intelligence & Planning, pp. 473–487
Parr, R.	Royalty Rates for Licensing Intellectual Property	2007	John Wiley & Sons, Inc.
Perrier, R.	Brand licensing	1998	In Brands (pp. 104–113). Palgrave Macmillan, London

(Continued)

TABLE 2.1 (Continued)

Author	Title	Year	Publisher
Prajit, G.	Protecting intellectual property in the Metaverse: Challenges, opportunities and recent case laws	2023	Voices, Tech, TOI
Raugust, K.	The Licensing Business Handbook	2004	EPM Communications, Inc.
Robinson, A. B., Tuli, K. R. and Kohli, A. K.	Does brand licensing increase a licensor's shareholder value	2015	Management Science, 61(6), pp. 1436–1455
Stone, M.	The Power of Licensing: Harnessing Brand Equity	2018	The American Bar Association

2. The Strategic Side of Brand Licensing

Licensing agreements are operations of value co-creation both for the licensor and for the licensee. The licensor has the opportunity to extend its brand into new product categories, expanding product portfolios, targets, distribution channels and geographic areas with a limited investment compared to a direct one. The licensee expands its product range, leveraging the strength of the licensor's brand, reputation and image, thus enhancing its market positioning. The licensed property should fit with the licensee's products, in terms of demographic target, corporate philosophies and the goals of the parties (Raugust, 2004). There are several strategic issues to manage in brand licensing. They include: the ways to implement it, the role players involved in the brand licensing process, the licensed product flow, the royalty payments flow and a licensing program setting.

The licensing agreement can be implemented in three ways: the *licensing-out*, the *licensing-in* and *cross-licensing*. *Licensing-out* consists in granting patent and/or know-how licenses in addition to use of the brand in order to provide the brand owner with incremental income to the revenues deriving from the manufacture and direct sale of the products. Weber®, in partnership with Sazerace and B&G Foods, announced on August 17, 2023, the launch of three new Weber® Seasoning Blends inspired by the flavors of some of Sazerac Company's most popular spirits, including Fireball™ Cinnamon Whisky, Buffalo Trace™ Bourbon and Southern Comfort™ Whiskey. Sazerac is one of America's oldest family-owned, privately held distillers with operations in the US. Each seasoning blend is non-alcoholic and has been meticulously crafted to capture the flavors iconic to each spirit brand. Weber®, the licensed brand behind the range of grilling seasoning blends, has been an innovator within grilling spices for years, designed to perform exceptionally on the grill, delivering delicious meat, veggies and sides. Brandgenuity, the licensing agency for Sazerac, brokered the agreement between B&G Foods and Sazerac. All three seasoning varieties will be available at Kroger stores (Seavy, 2023). *Licensing-in* is the acquisition of a trademark, patented or unpatented technologies or know-how by a company. Luxottica Group is a leader in the design, production and distribution of high-end, luxury and sports sunglasses and eyeglasses. It holds a portfolio both of owned brands – with Ray-Ban, Oakley, Vogue Eyewear, Persol, Oliver Peoples, Arnette, Costa del Mar and Alain Mikli – and under license with the brands Giorgio Armani, Burberry, Bulgari, Chanel, Dolce&Gabbana, Ferrari, Michael Kors, Prada, Coach, Ralph Lauren, Tiffany & Co., Valentino and Versace. In 2018, Luxottica Group and Tiffany renewed their eyewear licensing agreement, which provides for the exclusive design, production and worldwide distribution of optical frames and sunglasses under the Tiffany & Co brand until December 31, 2027 (Reyes, 2017).

Cross-licensing is the mutual granting of licenses between two businesses, thus reducing the risk of mutual lawsuits. It can lead to an increase in sales and market share by acquiring new target customers for both partners. The partnership between Gucci and The North Face is an example of a cross-licensing program in the field of fashion. In 2021 Gucci and The North Face launched a licensing program that includes a collection of items of clothing, footwear, luggage, sleeping bags and tents with a sustainable footprint. The partnership aims to strengthen the eco-friendly image, thus expanding the customer base interested in products that use nylon fabrics obtained from regenerated materials. The values that bind the two partners evoke the spirit of adventure, open spaces, the purity of nature, the partnership between aesthetics and functionality, and the achievement of the highest peaks thanks to the ability to overcome physical, social and emotional obstacles (Portee, 2020).

There are several role players involved in the brand licensing process. As a minimum there are four actors: the *brand owner* (licensor), the *manufacturer* (licensee), the *retailer* and the *consumer*. The *brand owner*, which is known as the licensor, is the company choosing to license its brand out. The next participant is the *manufacturer* which chooses to license the brand from the brand owner, which is known as the licensee. Once the relationship has been established, the licensee (manufacturer) then talks to *retailers* to create a program in their retail stores. After the retailer agrees to host the brand in its store, the focus shifts to the *consumer* because consumers drive the consumption and success of all consumer brands. The consumers are the ones that make the final decision, have a personal relationship with the brands, buy the merchandise that is sold to the retailers by the manufacturer and use their wallets to make the brands successful. Since licensing is a long-term contract, the licensor establishes a long-term cooperative relationship with the licensee. We use an example where the brand owner is a well-known brand in sportswear, and the manufacturer is the one who produces athletic apparel. The brand owner is a powerful brand that started in running shoes and has expanded into a tremendous number of categories today. The brand owner goes to a manufacturer who produces athletic apparel in an effort to expand their brands. In response, the manufacturer agrees to license the brand because they are familiar with the licensor's reputation and know that this will benefit both parties. So, the brand owner along with the manufacturer consummate a binding relationship. Once the relationship has been established the licensee (manufacturer), then talks to retailers to create a program in their retail stores. Since the licensor is well-known by many, the retailer agrees and then arranges a relationship where they purchase the product and stock it on their shelves. After the retailer agrees to host the brand in its store, the focus shifts to the consumer because consumers drive the consumption and success of all consumer brands. The consumers are the ones that make the final decision, have the personal relationship with the brands, buy the merchandise that is sold to the retailers by the manufacturer and use their wallets to make the brands successful.

The licensed product flows start once the relationship is consummated. The licensee will start to develop concepts of what the product should look like. When these concepts are approved, prototypes will then be created for review and decisions will be made to reject or approve each prototype. Next, the final production run samples are tested to ensure that the product meets all quality and safety standards. In the final step, both the licensor and the licensee agree on the finished product to ensure the product is safe to be sold and placed into the retail market. Thereby, the product is available to be sold to the consumer. That's the flow of how the licensed products are created (Figure 2.1).

Royalty payments flow is another part of the brand licensing relationship. It includes the payment of royalties, the percentage royalty rate, the unit price, the order size, the retail revenue, the wholesale revenue, the product markup and the retailer's gross margin. A license agreement requires the licensee to pay a fee (a royalty) for the brand's use. The lump-sum payment consists of a fixed amount paid in one installment or in a series of regular installments (quarterly). As an alternative to paying in cash, the licensor may also receive a share of the licensee's company or the possibility of buying it at a reduced price. The percentage payout varies based on the strength of the brand and the success achieved by the licensee. The percentage is applied on the sale price or on the number of units sold. Mixed payments envisage an immediate initial payment and a deferred payment, consisting of royalties or periodic payments of a fixed type. In most cases, licensing agreements include a fixed part known as the "guaranteed minimum" which has the purpose of guaranteeing the licensee for the investment and the licensor for the expenses incurred for the contract conclusion, and a variable represented by the royalties on sales (Battersby, 2019). The following example explains how the payment flow works. The consumer buys a branded polo shirt at a retailer for $50. When the entire initial shipment of 200,000 polo shirts is sold at the retailer's stores, that constitutes $10M worth of sold merchandise, which the retailer receives from consumers. Of that, the retailer paid $5M for that product received from the manufacturer who licensed the brand. The retailer marked it up 100 percent to get a 50 percent margin. That $5M of merchandise that was bought by the retailer from the manufacturer generates $500,000 in royalties for the licensor based on a 10 percent royalty rate, which the manufacturer agreed to pay for the brand. Once the purchase order (PO) from the retailer is issued to the manufacturer, who licensed the brand and the payment is made, the manufacturer will pay the licensor $500,000 in royalties for the merchandise that they sold. That's how the payment flow works (Figure 2.2).

Brand licensing program setup is about planning and implementing all activities (including role player identification, due diligence, SWOT analysis, negotiation agreement content, business plan), according to a timeline and step-by-step, starting months before the licensed product is commercialized or launched.

| Product categories selection to be licensed by Licensors | License negotiation between Licensors or Agents and Licensees | Concepts, prototypes and final production samples developed by Licensees to be submitted to Licensors for approval | Licensors' approval of licensed products for sale | Licensees' sales of approved licensed products in authorized retail channels |

FIGURE 2.1 Licensed Product Flow

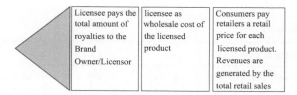

| Licensee pays the total amount of royalties to the Brand Owner/Licensor | licensee as wholesale cost of the licensed product | Consumers pay retailers a retail price for each licensed product. Revenues are generated by the total retail sales |

FIGURE 2.2   Royalty Payment Flow

INTERVIEW TO ALEX LOCKE ON THE STRATEGIC SIDE OF BRAND LICENSING

In this interview of December 1, 2022, Pete Canalichio, brand strategist and licensing expert, discussed with Alex Locke, attorney, licensing and NFT expert, about how to manage licensing in the digital world. The interview took place over Zoom with Pete located in his office in Atlanta and Alex in his office located in New York City. The interview lasted approximately one hour. Here, an excerpt of the interview is reported (Table 2.2). The central topic is to understand how brand licensing works and how important it is from a business perspective.

TABLE 2.2 The Strategic Side of Brand Licensing in the Opinion of an Expert

Topic	Expert's Answers
Differences in brand and software licensing	The analysis on using licensing for branding is no different than for software. It is possible to use the same analysis whether it's for brand licensing for consumer goods or for software licensing.
	A company that wants to build an app to further their social engagement in their community was faced with the questions, "Do they hire developers and an internal team to build it out and own it, or should they license it out?" and "What are the pros and cons?" "Why does it work for this existing use case?" So, the company can use licensing as it shifts the cost to the licensee. They have lower profit margins but less exposure both from the legal liability as well as investment and risk. Someone else bears the burden; the downside is that they have a smaller profit margin than they would if they built the app. Depending on how they negotiate and structure the relationship, they may not own the underlying software which may have inherent value in and of itself.
	Using this process for a brand requires a similar analysis to what is used with software licensing.
The benefit of entering a category via licensing	Is it worth it to hire a whole staff dedicated to licensing, or instead develop the manufacturing capabilities [for the categories you wish to create] and go through a whole new arena and deal with the learning curve as well as the investment? Licensing is a way to kind of dip your toes [in the water] and try it out. Of course, there's inherent risk in anything, especially anything featuring your brand. But you know if a product doesn't sell well, it's the licensee that is the one holding the inventory and losing the money. The brand owner has less skin in the game and less exposure.

(Continued)

TABLE 2.2 (Continued)

Topic	Expert's Answers
Using licensing as an experimentation tool	I've seen people using licensing where the outcome is unknown. They know their brand works really well in [one] area and they want to try it in a different territory or a different product line or a different offering. They are not sure if it's going to work so [they] do a few years term with a licensee to test the water. If it ends up being a huge money maker and really successful, then they can make the calculated decision it's worth it. The best thing is using licensing in this new vertical and if successful, then bringing it in-house once the license term ends. Or the licensor realizes the relationship's great and says, "Let's just keep it running and expand it and expand this licensee's product grant and/or bring on new licenses."
Licensing alliances between brand owners and manufacturers	Many people don't know what this licensing industry is about and don't know how to even approach it. Then it'll be somebody like you or me who says, "Well I hear what you're saying but instead of building that thing, have you ever considered licensing as a different solution?" Oftentimes, the answer is what are you talking about? They don't even know what you are talking about. At that point you start the whole education process. When I was at Brandgenuity, I worked on the BMW account. BMW is an automobile manufacturer. This company makes cars; however, when you see BMW's logo on any BMW product that is not an actual automobile that comes off the dealership lot, whether it be the car in a video game, a tracksuit with a logo, kids driving little cars, you know that's outside of their manufacturing core capabilities. These products are licensed. From the licensees' perspective, they might have a great product, but it doesn't have recognizability, so they know that adding the BMW brand to their product makes it stand out on the shelf. For the licensors, they don't have the capabilities to make that product available or the distribution network to get it to retail in that niche. The licensee has the product, and the licensor has the brand, so it's a perfect marriage.
Licensing is hidden in plain sight	As the leader of your organization, start to ask your organization, "Hey, why are we not pursuing licensing?" And they will begin to learn about it from that perspective, versus, "Oh, I bumped into this attorney named Alex, and I asked him what he did and he told me all about this thing [called licensing]." I mean it's just crazy. People don't realize that half the things in their home are licensed. That could be a good intro or preface. It's like you would never think that. The craziest example that I learned through working in this industry is that one of the licensees that I used to work with sells bulk mini shampoos to hotels and resort companies. A guest might see Revlon shampoo in some resort in Mexico, or wherever they are, and that's not even made by Revlon, its licensed. Or a person goes into Home Depot to buy a Caterpillar hammer. The person assumes that they [Caterpillar] make it, but they don't, also licensed. They make tractors which are extremely durable and there's a synergy. That's why I love talking to folks who are experts in this industry because I know that together we can create something really of value. It's cool that you have this brand annuity background which makes what you do even that much more beneficial.

Topic	Expert's Answers
Aligning Brand extensions via licensing with a brand's positioning	You have to know where you are in the food chain. A lot of times the luxury brands are loss leaders, and the less prestigious brands or product offerings generate more revenue. You have to be honest with yourself and identify what your brand stands for, what your brand is. It happens all the time where I hear some non "Prestige Brands" say, "We're aspirational." It's like, "No you're not, and that's fine." You're wasting a lot of time and effort barking up the wrong tree when there is a unique licensor and a licensee for everyone. Identify what your brand stands for, what are your core values. Be honest about them and don't always just copy whatever the current trend is. Align those interests with the licensee and vice versa with the heart and soul of your organization or your company or your brand. Both the licensor and licensee need to have the same general core values.
How video streaming has impacted the licensed products sales	A great case study is Netflix and their original content which they license. They would always ask for the viewership metrics. It was a black box up until recently. It's a very big shift right. If you think about streaming, you could talk about how it is affecting licensing in the entertainment space. This is probably anecdotal but I'm sure there's data to support it. Consider the show Stranger Things for example. Prior to the streaming model, that season could last the whole year. When it's over the consumer is waiting for more licensed products. Today, you don't have time to finish and continue that cycle. Let's say the new season of Stranger Things comes out tomorrow. Half the viewership can finish streaming it in 24 hours and then by the time the licensed product gets to market, Netflix is already in the middle of bringing the sixth show that comes after it. So Stranger Things doesn't have the longevity that it did historically, because Netflix drove this model, the streaming model, to the world. That is why you're starting to see streaming platforms coming out with shows on a weekly or more incremental interval.

3. The Licensor Side of Brand Licensing

A brand owner can use two options to extend a brand using external resources. The first is to acquire a company that is currently commercializing the product. The advantages of this option include having the manufacturing, marketing and selling of the product under one (the brand owner's) roof, which means quality control and costs can be more easily managed. One of the disadvantages of acquiring a company to extend the brand is that the brand owner needs to have sufficient access to capital to complete the transaction. Additionally, this external option can require a significant amount of time to consummate, and even if the transaction is completed, there still could be inadequate resources allocated for marketing the product, thereby restricting the brand owner's ability to move forward successfully. Finally, the integration of an acquired company can often be tedious and difficult to accomplish (Hitt et al., 2012). Many acquisitions end in failure.

The second option a brand owner could choose to extend their brand is to license it to a business selling the product in the desired category. Companies license their brands for a variety of reasons related to the opportunity both of unlocking their brands' latent value and of satisfying pent-up demand while maintaining control over an original creation. Through licensing, brand owners have the ability to enter new categories practically overnight, gaining them immediate brand presence on store shelves and often in the media (Stone & Trebbien, 2019). The advantages of this option are the investment risks are lower and the business, or licensee, possesses the capability to not only manufacture the product but also market it. The licensee also possesses the necessary relationships with distributors and retailers to make a success of the program. Each licensing program benefits the licensor by allowing the brand to connect with fans in more ways, which not only builds brand equity but also drives royalty revenue. Euroitalia (www.euroitalia.it) is a family business leader in the distribution and sale of Italian Made perfumes. Founded in 1978 by Giovanni Sgariboldi, EuroItalia collaborates with fashion houses and stylists to translate market trends into new fragrances to be marketed all over the world. Several partnerships link EuroItalia with the major fashion brands, including Versace, Moschino, Missoni, Michael Kors, Dsquared2, as licensee of men's/women's fragrances to exploit the potential value of fashion brands in related business by targeting valuable market segments interested in outfits of a specific brand. L'Amy America is a company of the ILG group, which produces and sells brand-licensed luxury accessories through an extensive worldwide distribution network. The L'Amy America portfolio is made up of international luxury brands, such as sunglasses and eyeglasses under the Kenzo, Vespa, Made In Italy, Cerruti and Canali brands (Guyot, 2017), watch collections, jewelry and leather goods branded Nina Ricci, Christian Lacroix, Jean Paul Gaultier and Timberland.

The benefits that make licensing so attractive to brand owners can be summarized in the following points:

- Test drive new businesses or geographical markets with minimal risk.
- Collect royalty revenue in exchange for the right to use the brand.
- Increase their overall marketing support for the core business.
- Execute a competitive strike.
- Gain strategic knowledge.

To Test Drive New Businesses or Geographical Markets with Minimal Risk

By partnering with a third-party manufacturer or service provider, a brand owner can try new businesses or move itself into new countries with a smaller upfront investment than by building and staffing its own operations (Belu & Caragin, 2008). Since the product manufacturing and distribution are handled by the licensee – the company with the product expertise – there is very little licensor engagement with the product and there is no inventory commitment.

Collect Royalty Revenue in Exchange for the Right to Use the Brand

While usually not the most important reason, licensing generates revenue from a minimum guarantee and through royalty payments. Guarantees are usually determined on an annual basis and calculated as a percentage of the anticipated per-annum royalty. Royalty payments are typically calculated as a percentage of wholesale revenue. As long as the brand is protected and the licensing program is properly administered, no general manager would knowingly turn away the healthy injection these payments bring to his/her bottom line.

Increase Their Overall Marketing Support for the Core Business

Another potential benefit to the licensor could include access to knowledge and insights held by the licensee. The licensee may know a manufacturing or marketing technique that can be incorporated into the licensor's go-to-market strategy. Licensors have an inside purview of what happens throughout their extended licensing organization and how their licensees perform. In many instances, the licensee will be required to provide marketing dollars to support the licensed category, which is important for the success of the license. This marketing spend, in turn, provides additional overall brand presence (Cross, 2015). For example: (1) if a licensee promotes its product in a weekly circular and gains an end-aisle display, the advertising and display not only generate product sales for the licensee, but they also promote the brand owner's core products. (2) An array of branded toys or apparel tied to a movie, sitting on a store shelf, also helps to promote the movie. (3) A sports fan who wears a sweatshirt with the logo of her favorite team expresses her enthusiasm about the team, but also subtly promotes the sports, the league and the team to anyone walking by. (4) Seeing a store display of glassware carrying a well-known beer logo like Guinness or walking into a neighbor's home and seeing the glasses on his bar reinforces the brand image, supporting the brand's overall marketing.

Execute a Competitive Strike

For licensors who know their brand can enter a category that is controlled by their competitor, licensing can be a smart and effective way to combat a rival in a category core to their business (Sałamacha, 2020). By taking the offensive, the licensor will in turn take the competitor's eye off of their own core business. For example, what if Adidas licensed a shoe manufacturer to compete directly against Cole Haan shoes with Nike AirTM?

Gain Strategic Knowledge

As many licensees are experts in their own right, they offer the licensor access to intangibles such as intellectual property (through licensing inbound), product design and marketing expertise, supply chain management, new customer relationships and strategic alliances. Licensors get a preview of any newly created technology or innovative products that the licensee intends to develop with the licensor's brand. The licensor is granted direct access to the strong and enduring supplier, distributor and retail relationships that the licensee has built over time. This affords the licensor the opportunity to create its own relationships in those channels or markets that were unobtainable previously. Having insight into this knowledge can prove to be profitable to their ongoing business (Mottner & Johnson, 2000). As true partners, a licensor and a licensee can hold forums to exchange ideas that not only grow the licensed category but also improve other areas of both companies' businesses.

In addition, for brand owners (particularly those doing business in the global marketplace), licensing and registering the brands in multiple markets is a way to protect the brand from being used by others without authorization. When licensing first started at Coca-Cola, it was run by the legal department specifically to protect the company's trademarks in the categories they chose to license throughout the world. Some licensors see licensing as an opportunity to "test" the viability of a new category without having to make a major investment in new manufacturing processes, machinery or facilities. In a well-run licensing program, the brand owner maintains control over the brand image and how it's portrayed (via the approvals process and other contractual structures), positioning itself to reap the benefit of additional revenue (royalties) and brand exposure through product displayed through new channels and incremental shelf space. For example, Rubbermaid gained additional revenue and brand presence by licensing kitty litter containers that are sold in the mass channel core to Rubbermaid, and in specialty pet shops core to United Pet Group, the licensee. Finally, by licensing their brands, companies are able to satisfy consumer needs in categories that are not core to their business.

One disadvantage of licensing is that the brand owner (licensor) routinely shares its know-how, causing the licensor potentially to create a future competitor when the licensing agreement expires. Besides the risk of losing its know-how, the licensor also faces the danger that the licensee could damage the image of the brand or the reputation of the company (Wiedmann & Ludewig, 2008), if it does not respect or adhere to the pre-established quality standards or if it acts in a harmful way. This would negatively impact customers' perception of the brand and threaten trust in the product and service offered. Another disadvantage of licensing is that the licensor must relinquish some control of their brand and potential profit margin to the licensee.

THE LAUNCH OF THE IPOD

When Apple launched the iPod a number of years ago, they revolutionized the way in which people listen to their music. The iPod was so successful that its quick acceptance created an immediate need for accessories such as armbands, adapters and auto-chargers. Apple could have chosen to manufacture and distribute these accessories themselves. Instead, Apple decided that these accessories were not core to their business expertise and therefore chose to satisfy the need through licensing. By licensing the iPod brand, Apple enabled a tremendous number of companies to produce all kinds of terrific products to make the iPod more user-friendly and to enhance the listening experience. Examples of licensed products for the iPod include the Bose Sound System with iPod docking station, the Nike+ running shoe, auto adaptor kits, armbands and many other products. All these accessories are sold by licensees.

THE M&M'S BRAND EXPANSION

M&M's is one of the most loved brands in the marketplace. Their advertising is best in class; they portray feelings of fun and happiness, and when consumed, they provide good experiences to the consumer. M&M Mars, the owner of the M&M's brand, understands that limiting the brand to food products alone would mean the brand is underoptimization. To avoid this and increase its growth, M&M Mars licensed the M&M's brand to a third-party manufacturer to produce iconic characters and jackets. In other cases, the M&M's brand licensing team has decided to license in brands the company does not own. For instance, M&M's chose to license a variety of brands to put on their candy products, such as the NFL. This allows consumers to go to the M&M's website, create an account and customize their M&M's with their favorite NFL team. So, if a fan of the Philadelphia Eagles wanted M&M's with the Eagles logo on them, that consumer could do that. Through licensing, M&M's is able to connect with a wide array of consumers in the way those consumers want to experience the brand. For M&M's, these types of licensing arrangements propelled the brand out in the marketplace in the categories they would not be in otherwise. This makes the brand more consumable and enjoyable by brand fans and enthusiasts.

THE ANPANMAN BRAND EXPANSION

Anpanman, a fictional character created by Takashi Yanase and one of the most popular animated children's cartoon series in Japan, was inspired by a soldier struggling to survive in World War II. Anpanman was introduced as a series of books in 1968 and became a television series in Japan in 1988. By 2006, more than 50 million Anpanman books were sold in Japan and Anpanman became the most popular fictional character in Japan for the under 12-year-old market. Anpanman has been heavily merchandised, appearing on licensed products, including apparel, video games, toys and snack foods.

4.   The Licensee Side of Brand Licensing

After having a better understanding of how brand owners benefit by allowing their brands to be extended via licensing, we look at how manufacturers and service providers (licensees) can also benefit. For manufacturers and service providers (licensees), the list of benefits is equally extensive and includes gaining marketing power, credibility and legitimacy, acquiring brand owner knowledge and experience, improving efficiency through the licensing plans implementation and increasing chances of securing other licenses (Santo, 2015). That is why this strategy is so powerful.

Licensees borrow the rights to a brand to build into their merchandise, but traditionally they do not share ownership in it. Having access to major national and global brands, and the associated logos and trademarks, gives the licensee significant benefits they previously did not possess. The most important of these is the marketing power the brand brings to the licensee's products. Building a brand from scratch can take years, millions of dollars and a lot of investments. The company which licenses a brand gains immediate access to all the positive name and image building that went before it. The licensee also takes with them the reputation of the licensor (Lewis, 2002). Often this "halo" effect can translate into many intangible and immeasurable benefits such as returned calls, an agreement to meet or simply the implication of quality. Specifically, the main benefits are the following:

- Achieve instantaneous recognition and credibility.
- Enhance their authenticity and legitimacy.

- Reduce in-house costs.
- Gain access into new distribution channels.
- Enter new regions.
- Acquire strategic knowledge.
- Obtain other licenses more easily.
- Add value to the business.

Achieve Instantaneous Recognition

Licensing offers immediate credibility and recognition, enabling licensees to enter new markets while enhancing sales of their core products (Canalichio, 2018). Consider an unbranded tee shirt manufacturer with specialty printing capabilities. While they may have a good network, they are relatively unknown beyond that. Through licensing they could be selling branded tee shirts; they could be, for example, an official Disney licensee of Mickey Mouse and Winnie the Pooh. Having the Disney license means immediate and instantaneous global recognition. The value of this recognition cannot be measured, but the sales the manufacturer will make certainly can.

Enhance Their Authenticity and Legitimacy

Licensees also gain authenticity and legitimacy through well-known brands that consumers trust. If a company is a third-party manufacturer who doesn't have a recognizable brand or well-known in the marketplace, having a terrific innovative product does not enhance sales without brand awareness. When bringing a brand that is recognizable and loved by consumers on sales calls, that credibility lends itself to a potentially successful solution. Consider the videogame manufacturer who has developed an amazing soccer game. They have presented their game to a number of retailers, but all have turned them down. If, however, they can license the FIFA World Cup trademark, they stand to gain immediate legitimacy and authenticity to their game (Weszka, 2014). In fact, many retailer buyers will tell a manufacturer that if they had a recognized brand, they would issue a purchase order. Similarly, a maker of automotive parts or accessories will license specific car brands such as Toyota or Ford specifically to establish in the consumer's mind that its products will work seamlessly with the cars of the parent brand. These are then purchased by automotive distributors, service shops and the brand's owners driving substantial incremental revenue.

Reduce In-House Costs

A manufacturer or service provider which acquires the rights to license a brand often gains the licensor's preferred pricing by its suppliers (Eisenmann, 2008). This can include commodities, such as resin, shipping and creative services. In addition, they gain access to the licensor's style guide, which provides them with most of the imagery and artwork they need to design their products. Having the style guide not only assists the licensee with design time, it streamlines the approval process and ensures their products have the same look as the other manufacturers or service providers which have licensed the brand.

Gain Access into New Distribution Channels

Taking on a license can help manufacturers and service providers gain access to new distribution channels (Hirt & Willmott, 2014). For example, a manufacturer may have an established private label business selling into the mass merchandise channel. By licensing the rights to a mid-tier brand, they could gain access into department stores (that wouldn't carry the private label brand) and double their revenue.

Enter New Regions

A door mat manufacturer based in Germany and selling its product in Europe may be able to enter the US market by licensing a major household brand like Better Homes & Gardens (Frey et al., 2015). The Better Homes & Gardens brand can give them entry into the channels they currently are selling other categories of products. In some instances, the licensees pool their products to create an integrated program, which can be appealing to some retailer buyers.

Acquire Strategic Knowledge

Through licensing the company acquires strategic knowledge from the brand owner that can prove to be profitable in its ongoing business (Chesbrough, 2006). Licensees gain access to intangibles such as the licensor's subject matter expertise in areas where they are not proficient such as marketing, supply chain management, customs and so on. In addition, manufacturers and service providers can benefit from the licensor's databases and libraries which can include a variety of topics including market research, manufacturing and product design (Siegel & Wright, 2015). As partners, licensor and licensee are not limited to these areas but can identify where each other's strengths are and tap into them.

Obtain Other Licenses More Easily

There are intangible and tangible benefits associated with brand licensing. Once a licensee acquires one license, they will almost automatically gain approval from other brand owners wishing to extend their brands into new categories (Richardson, 2014). A manufacturer which has secured a license with a great brand is, in fact, considered a better company and probably is going to be valued higher by the next licensors. For example, a pin licensee of Major League Baseball (MLB) will have an easier time acquiring the rights to the National Hockey League or the National Basketball Association because these brand owners know the licensee meets the standards for MLB and already has an understanding of the licensing process.

Add Value to the Business

Gaining the rights to one of the world's great brands can add instantaneous value to an organization (Aitken et al., 2000). This could be an important consideration when the owners are considering selling the company. More and more brand owners are aware of this and are requiring they approve the new management before automatically authorizing the continuation of the license. In addition, the brand owner may require a payment recognizing the increase in value upon the sale of the company.

CO-LICENSING PROGRAMS – THE PARTNERSHIPS BETWEEN PRADA AND ADIDAS

In the field of fashion, examples of co-licensing programs are the partnerships between Prada and Adidas. Prada and Adidas have kicked off a long-term licensing program, the most recent of which is January 13, 2022, with the global launch of the "Adidas for Prada Re-Nylon" collection. The collection includes clothing, accessories, bags and footwear, high-end fitness clothing, sweatshirts and special versions of Adidas Forum High and Low sneakers. The line integrates luxury and sustainability through the use of Re-Nylon tissue in production. It is a regenerated fabric obtained from the recycling of plastic materials recovered in the oceans. The two partners, who operate in distinct segments of the clothing and accessories market (respectively, the luxury segment and sport one), share the values of protecting the planet, enhancing people and culture. The collection intends to penetrate the luxury sportswear segment, positioning itself with products that integrate innovation in techniques, sustainability, Adidas' expertise in high-performance sportswear, and Prada's vision of luxury and refinement.

5. Running the Licensing Marathon

Brand licensing can be beneficial for both brands and licensees if done in a step-by-step manner. Building an effective and enduring brand licensing program is akin to running a multi-stage marathon (Chernev, 2020). In addition to a lot of training, efforts and consistency, a strategy is required to keep a program running for a long time. So, the licensing marathon idea powerfully conveys what is needed to keep a program running for a long time. We have divided the brand licensing process into eight steps (Figure 2.3):

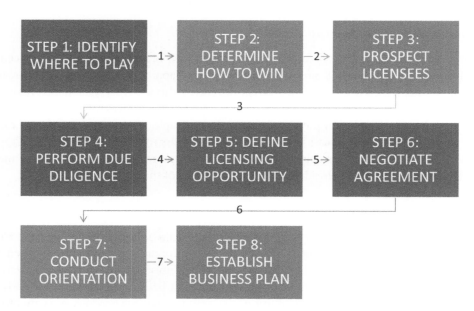

FIGURE 2.3   Brand Licensing Process in Steps

STEP 1: Identify Where to Play

STEP 2: Determine How to Win

STEP 3: Prospect Licensees

STEP 4: Perform Due Diligence

STEP 5: Define Licensing Opportunity

STEP 6: Negotiate Agreement

STEP 7: Conduct Orientation

STEP 8: Establish Business Plan

The brand licensing process starts several months prior to the commercialization or launch of the licensed product. Figure 2.4 gives a timeline of each of the processes listed in Figure 2.3. Missing crucial deadlines such as a line review can push the product launch out.

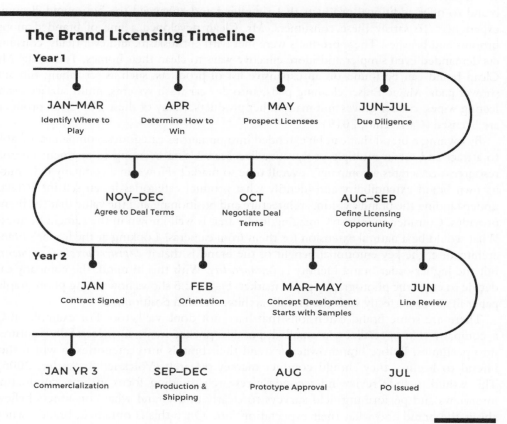

The Brand Licensing Timeline

Year 1

JAN–MAR	APR	MAY	JUN–JUL
Identify Where to Play	Determine How to Win	Prospect Licensees	Due Diligence

NOV–DEC	OCT	AUG–SEP
Agree to Deal Terms	Negotiate Deal Terms	Define Licensing Opportunity

Year 2

JAN	FEB	MAR–MAY	JUN
Contract Signed	Orientation	Concept Development Starts with Samples	Line Review

JAN YR 3	SEP–DEC	AUG	JUL
Commercialization	Production & Shipping	Prototype Approval	PO Issued

FIGURE 2.4 Timeline of the Brand Licensing Process

STEP 1: Identify Where to Play

When consumers become delighted by a particular brand experience, they begin to bond emotionally with the brand. They become brand loyalists and advocates – buying the brand more often and recommending it to others. This behavior serves to build the brand's reputation. Consumers will often purchase a brand for the first time because of its reputation. The brand, therefore, adds value and certainty to an otherwise unknown product. The stronger a brand's reputation, the higher the value of the brand and the greater revenue it will drive for its owner. Prospective licensees want to license brands with the strongest reputation, as these are the brands consumers demand and retailers prefer most. The stronger the brand, the higher the likelihood that retailers will buy the licensed products and that they will be subsequently purchased by consumers. Brand loyalists and advocates look to their preferred brands to deliver new and better option products for them to buy. When this occurs, the brand gains permission to extend into categories that complement its original offering. This is known as brand extension. For example, the Mr. Clean brand, owned by P&G, was launched in 1963 as the first household liquid cleaner. Over time, the brand gained a strong reputation for its ability to clean effectively on a variety of surfaces. By delighting its consumers, Mr. Clean built significant brand loyalty and allegiance. When asked, consumers told the Mr. Clean brand team that they expected the Mr. Clean brand to offer additional products that simplified and enhanced the household cleaning experience. To satisfy these consumers, Mr. Clean developed a line of branded mops, brooms and brushes. These products were met with enthusiasm, and eventually, consumers demanded even simpler and more effective ways to clean their homes. Today, the Mr. Clean brand can be found on an expansive list of products, such as scrubbing tub and shower pads, Magic Eraser cleaning pads, auto dry car wash systems, multi-surface disinfecting wipes, rubber gloves and many other products. Many of these Mr. Clean products are licensed (Canalichio, 2019).

By owning a brand that can be extended into numerous categories, companies are able to attract and retain multiple prospective licensees. Using licensing to augment internal resources accelerates a company's overall time to market. How can a company determine its own brand extendibility and identify what product categories it can sell in? It takes understanding the brand's vision, architecture and positioning and the value that the brand provides. Consider an industry imaging leader that is well-known in the camera business. What would be a natural extension for them from cameras? Looking at the leader's brand architecture, the key emotional benefit of the brand is that it *captures precious moments*, but the higher-order brand identity is *immortality*. With this in mind, the company can decide to enter the photography paper market. Figure 2.5 shows how selling photography paper fits in so perfectly with the brand's architecture and positioning.

There are some brand extensions that have not done well, too. For example, BiC, a company that specializes in small disposable pocket items unsuccessfully ventured into perfumes. Before brand owners extend their brands into categories in which they intend to license, they should conduct market research (Völckner & Sattler, 2006). This would include reviewing secondary research, holding focus groups, conducting interviews and performing field surveys to clearly understand what consumers believe about the brand and what their expectations are. Once this is obtained, brand owners will be able to identify suitable categories in which to extend. Each category should

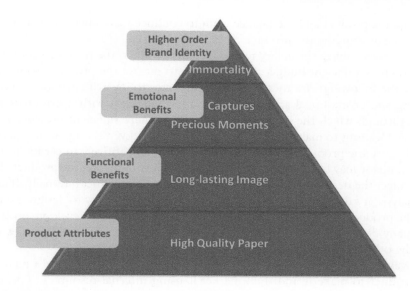

FIGURE 2.5   Brand Architecture of Industry Imaging Company

then be evaluated on the prominence of brand associations, favorability of associations inferred by the extension and uniqueness of association from the new category. Once the list of possible extensions has been trimmed, brand owners should then conduct an industry and competitive analysis of the category. Specifically, research includes the size of the market, current competitors, industry growth rate and competitive nature. This analysis will enable the brand owner to determine whether it makes sense to even enter the category. One technique to use is a Strengths–Weaknesses–Opportunities–Threats (SWOT) analysis. This method is helpful in evaluating a business or a project from a strategic point of view.

STEP 2: Determine How to Win

Once the product category that satisfies the brand extension goals and creates positive associations for the licensor's brand has been identified, the next step is to determine how to go about executing the extension (Verma & Kumar, 2022). Since a marketing activity requires substantial resources, before a project is begun the brand owner determines whether the company has enough resources to complete the endeavor. So how could the brand owner determine the best way to go about entering the product category that has been selected?

A first step is to mobilize key departments within the organization to conduct their own due diligence. When contemplating entering a new product category, the first step is to determine whether the company has the competency to design, produce and market the product with internal resources. When we refer to internal resources, we are referring to either the company's manufacturing capability to produce the product or its ability to source the product competitively from one of its third-party suppliers. One way to accomplish this is to delegate the operations team to evaluate the competency of manufacturing or sourcing the product and the finance team to conduct a cost/benefit analysis of manufacturing versus sourcing the product.

If the analysis confers the ability to produce the product, the next step is to determine whether there is sufficient budget and capability to market the product. Some questions to ask are the following: Are there adequate resources to invest in product development, advertising and promotional activities? Do relationships exist with distributors and retail channels through which the product will be sold? Is there sufficient presence in enough geographic locations to make the brand extension viable? Even though it may be preferred to manufacture the product or source it and price it competitively to earn a healthy margin, the company may lack the resources or the capability to market the product effectively. This can affect the decision of whether to manufacture the product internally. If at the end of the analysis, it's determined that the company has the capability to design, produce and market the product, it should go ahead and proceed with product development. However, if a company does not possess the capability to produce the product internally, it should look at the other options available.

One way to extend the brand into the new category is to acquire a manufacturer of the product to make it and then market it using internal resources. This option is often harder than it seems. For one thing, a company would need extra cash flow to fund such a transaction. Also, acquiring new businesses is a time-consuming proposition. Potential target companies should be identified. Next, due diligence should be completed before negotiating a price. Once acquired, the company should be integrated within the existing company structure. Because of the lengthy process, critical time can be lost in launching the product. Even if a company decides to go with this option and the timing fits, it still may not have the marketing budget or the capability to go forward. The other way to extend the brand externally is to license the brand to a manufacturer of the product in the same category. As mentioned in previous chapters, there are several advantages to licensing a brand. To begin with, the manufacturer (or licensee) possesses the capability not only to manufacture the product but also to market it, having done so for unbranded items or lesser-known brands. They also possess the necessary relationships with distributors and retailers to make a success of the program. On the downside, the brand owner forgoes some control when they choose to license their brand. However, entering a new market via licensing has lower risk in terms of investment.

A licensor may decide to enter a new product category via licensing as the business evaluates its go-to-market strategies. Alternatively, the licensor's brand could be solicited by a manufacturer who believes its product would be a good fit for the brand. This would then start the process where the licensor's brand marketing team evaluates the product category of the manufacturer from a brand extendibility perspective. Figure 2.6 shows how the process would flow.

STEP 3: Prospect Licensees

Once the product category that best fits the brand extension plans has been identified and brand licensing is determined to be the most beneficial way to achieve this extension, it is time to scout for prospective licensees within the selected product category. Before shortlisting the licensees, it is important for the licensor to pull together a basic checklist

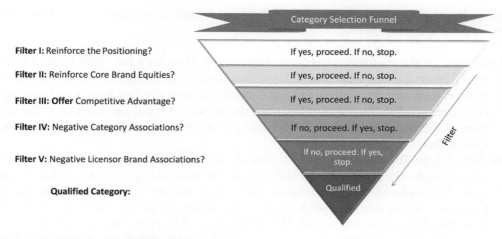

Category Selection Funnel	
Filter I: Reinforce the Positioning?	If yes, proceed. If no, stop.
Filter II: Reinforce Core Brand Equities?	If yes, proceed. If no, stop.
Filter III: Offer Competitive Advantage?	If yes, proceed. If no, stop.
Filter IV: Negative Category Associations?	If no, proceed. If yes, stop.
Filter V: Negative Licensor Brand Associations?	If no, proceed. If yes, stop.
Qualified Category:	Qualified

FIGURE 2.6 Category Qualification Process

of parameters in which to evaluate the licensees (Lotman, 2020). These parameters may include the following:

- Size – based on revenue and number of employees.
- Market share in the product category.
- Geographic reach.
- Current or previous licenses held.
- Financial strength.

Once the checklist has been developed, the next step is to identify companies that manufacture the selected product category. The most common sources of information are trade directories, trade magazines, trade shows and research companies like Hoovers, Dun and Bradstreet, Frost & Sullivan, and Vault Reports. Another way for the licensor to identify prospective licensees is to conduct primary research such as store walks. Once a comprehensive list of prospects is identified, these candidates should then be evaluated based on the parameters listed earlier. This will leave the licensor with a pool of qualified companies to investigate further. To make a licensing agreement a success, both parties should be willing to commit equal time and resources. Based on comprehensive interviews, the licensor would then shortlist the most qualified candidates with whom they desire to advance in the process.

STEP 4: Perform Due Diligence

This is the stage when the brand owner begins rigorously qualifying the prospective licensees to determine whether they will progress to the next phase. This stage involves conducting a comprehensive due diligence on the selected companies from a business, financial, legal and risk management perspective (Raugust, 2004). A good first step in this process is to develop a *licensee application* that requests all the information that is required from the licensee. The information from the application would substantiate whatever secondary research was garnered on the prospective licensee. A licensee application should typically include the following:

Legal check: Is the company a legitimate legal entity? How long have they been in business? Where are they incorporated? Are they doing business under a different name? What is their structure? Are they a shell corporation or do they have actual employees, assets and liabilities? Have they been the subject of any major lawsuits in the last three to five years? If so, what was the nature of the charges and how did the company resolve them?

Financial check: To understand fully the financial strength of an organization, it is important to obtain the prospective licensees' financial statements going back at least three years. Financial statements help assure the licensor that the licensee has the resources to commit to the licensing program from the beginning to the end of the contract. It is critical for a licensor to have this information. Therefore, this should be a non-negotiable item. Licensors should also conduct a credit check on all licensees. The credit check tells the licensor the timeliness and reliability of the prospective licensee to pay their bills. Given the systematic royalty payment requirements of the licensing contract, understanding the credit-worthiness of the prospective licensee is critical.

Business check: Is the company reputable in the selected product category? Do they possess any other brand licenses, or have they had them in the past? If so, what do their current or previous licensors have to say about the way they manage their licensing programs? What is their reputation in the marketplace? What do their current customers have to say about their reliability and serviceability? How well managed is the company? How eager are they to obtain a license? How collaborative do they seem? What are the estimated sales forecasts for the selected product, as well as the sales history, over the past three years?

Marketing check: What is the prospective licensee's market share in the selected product category? How long have they been selling the product? What is their rank by revenue, distribution, employees? Are they a market leader? What channels are they present in? How successfully have they been growing? What kind of product innovations have they launched in the past five years? What are their strengths? How well do they understand the marketplace and branding? How are they currently promoting their products?

Reference check: Reference checks are an important component of the due diligence process. Licensors should interview at least three buyers from among the retailers in which the prospective licensee intends to sell. This enables the licensor to quickly understand the quality of the company from a delivery, manufacturing, service, marketing and sales perspective. In addition, licensors should interview up to three licensors if the prospective licensee holds or has held other licenses. These interviews will enable the licensor to understand how effectively they can expect the prospective licensee to execute a licensing program.

Quality and compliance check: Does the licensee own their own manufacturing, or do they outsource it? If they source their product, how long have they been working with their manufacturers? Will they be able to meet the brand's quality expectations? How have these manufacturers performed on previous audits? Do they or can they meet the social and environmental compliance standards of the brand?

STEP 5: Define Licensing Opportunity

After completing the due diligence process, it's time to assess the size and scope of the opportunity presented (Santo, 2015). This requires the licensor to work with the selected candidate licensees to understand their strengths and determine whether the licensing opportunity is viable. To this end, the licensor can assess how well the candidate licensees will immerse themselves in the licensor's brand and fully understand its positioning and architecture. From this, it is important to understand the look and feel of the products they are proposing. As any designs or prototypes should incorporate the licensor's brand attributes, the licensor will evaluate how well the licensees have paid attention to the placement of the logo on the product, the material from which it is constructed and how the logo is affixed to the product. The licensee can request that the licensor provide them with the brand's style guide, so they have the required information to guide them. Simultaneously, the licensor should request that the candidate licensees develop three-year sales projections so they can assess the scope of the license. This forecast should be a conservative estimate of the sales the licensee thinks they can achieve and should be segmented by region, channel and Stock Keeping Units (SKUs). The sales projections should also include the number of new products the licensee thinks they will introduce each year.

The sales projections, provided by each of the shortlisted licensees, are compared with each other. The licensor then evaluates the proposals to assure they are viable, achievable and maximize the brand opportunity. For example, a prospective licensee who is number one in their category may only wish to dedicate a small portion of their business to the license, whereas the company which is number three in the category may be willing to convert all of their sales to the newly licensed brand. In this case the scope of the opportunity with the company ranked number three may be much larger than the company ranked number one, making them the preferred option. However, the licensor could challenge this proposal. They may determine that converting the entire breadth of a product from its current state to a branded state may not be achievable.

Once the sales projections have been vetted, the licensor should use these to rank the candidates. The size of sales targets can then be used as a guide when negotiating the following quantifiable deal terms: minimum sales targets, guaranteed royalty minimums and cash advances. As these deal terms are based on the forecasts developed by the licensees, they should not only be fair but also be robust and achievable. With these agreed terms in hand, the groundwork for the actual contract is prepared. The licensees and the licensors then are in a strong position to negotiate their licensing agreement.

STEP 6: Negotiate Agreement

The basis of the licensing opportunity has been prepared by the conservative sales estimates in the previous step. It is now time to establish the core deal terms. These parameters define the structure of the licensing agreement, and define such parameters as the term, where the licensed products will be sold, what royalty rate will be paid and what trademarks will be used. Because the value of these terms will be unique to every licensing agreement, they are negotiated between the licensor and prospective licensee (Simon & Battersby, 2011).

While each party inherently wants to arrive at the most favorable terms for their side, the best set of deal terms are those that allow both parties to achieve a successful long-term licensing program. Successful licensors keep the end in mind and practice win-win negotiating strategies. Similarly, successful licensees will have identified several choices of brands from which to acquire a license and will set limits on what deal terms they will accept, regardless of the brand. In these instances, both parties can shake hands on a set of terms they know will allow them both to be successful. These terms include rights to territories, channels, covered products and trademarks, work product, quality assurance standards, the licensing approval process, manufacturing facility approval, royalty rates, minimum guaranteed royalties and sales requirements. Understanding these terms and the commitments that will be made is crucial to an effective licensing agreement negotiation. As the deal terms are an integral part of the contract, they should be understood by all relevant members of the licensee's organization. The deal terms are reviewed by both parties, revised if necessary, and once both sides are comfortable with the terms, they are incorporated into the licensing agreement. Because licensing agreements will need to allow the licensor to fully protect their brand, they tend to be one-sided with significant provisions for termination. In most cases the standard agreement provisions are not negotiable, and as such, the licensing agreement is finalized and signed soon after the deal terms are agreed upon.

STEP 7: Conduct Orientation

The signing of the contract marks the beginning of a relationship (Stone, 2018). It is important for the licensee to get familiar with the licensor and the licensing program as much as possible, and it is the licensor's responsibility to make sure they provide the licensee with all the information they need. Well-run licensing programs require a formal orientation session shortly after the contract is signed. The orientation provides an opportunity for key members from the licensor and licensee's companies to meet and get to know each other. Attending from the licensor's side should be members from the licensing group, the brand group, product development and sales. Members attending from the licensee's side should include the general manager as well as representatives from product development, account management, sales and marketing. The licensor normally gives the licensee an overview of the brand story, brand architecture, brand positioning and category positioning. The licensor also takes the licensee through the product approval process, timelines and key terms in the licensing agreement. The orientation session also includes a review of all testing and auditing protocols.

Normally, the licensor will deliver a brand licensing style guide to the licensee at orientation. The style guide helps direct the licensee on how to use the brand logo and style elements when creating products, packaging and marketing collateral. In addition, the orientation session is used to walk the new licensee through the approval process. The licensees will need to be intimately familiar with the approval process if they wish to get their products approved quickly and efficiently.

STEP 8: Establish a Business Plan

After that both parties have signed an agreement and have made sure the licensee has a good understanding of the brand, it is important that the licensor give the licensee the right tools to be successful (Goldscheider & Gordon, 2006). Monitoring the licensee's business and ensuring that they set achievable targets enables them to make the maximum use of the license. The licensee should begin with developing a one-year business plan. The business plan should start with a firm understanding of the licensor's Brand and Category Positioning Statements. Key targets taken from the licensing contract should also be cited in the business plan. These include the minimum sales, the minimum guaranteed royalty payments and the royalty rate.

The business plan should also contain a clear understanding of the product development and commercialization timeline, the SKUs they plan to sell including any new products that they plan to develop and the key retailers where the licensee plans to sell their licensed product over the next year. The sales plan should be built by month, by retailer and, if applicable, by region. Projected royalties should be calculated based on the sales projections and reviewed against minimum guaranteed royalty payments to assess the robustness of the plan. Figure 2.7 shows a snapshot of what such a plan should contain.

Dashboard Reviews: On a monthly basis the licensor will review the business estimate against the plan. Thus, both the licensee and the licensor should track the actual sales and royalties versus those projected in the Annual Business Plan. Subsequent monthly projections should be laid out with justifications for any increases or decreases relative to the business plan and the most recent estimate. The results of this will be used to maximize opportunities within the calendar year and to develop the business plan for the following year. Similarly, there is a quarterly and an annual review that compare the sales performance with the previous quarter (or year).

Audits: Each licensing agreement provides the licensor with the right to audit its licensee. These audits include a review of the licensee's financial and product development records, as well as social compliance audits of its approved factories. Social compliance audits are conducted whenever a new licensee or facility is made part of a licensing program. In addition, business audits are performed routinely to ensure the licensee is complying with the terms of the agreement. Typically, audits are conducted by approved third parties. Any discrepancies found in a social compliance audit that can be harmful to the facility's employees should be resolved before the facility can be used. Others may be resolved on an ongoing basis. Licensee business audits that turn up any inconsistencies are reviewed for the seriousness of the finding. A discrepancy related to selling unapproved products or selling products in an unauthorized method could result in termination. In addition, most agreements include significant penalties for sales of unapproved or unauthorized products. Royalty requirements related to unauthorized sales typically are punitive in nature and could be as much as the sales value of the unauthorized licensed merchandise. Minor infractions are resolved by correcting the problem in a prudent and expeditious fashion.

Annual Business Plan

Licensee Name	Licensee #1	Year 2 Licensor Budget:	3,000,000
Submission Date:	Year 2	Year 2 Licensee Budget:	350,000
Royalty Rates (%):	5, 7.5, 10	Licensee Contribution:	12%
Minimum Guarantees:	100,000		
		Year 2 Licensor Estimate:	3,500,000
		Year 2 Licensee Estimate:	375,000
		Licensee Contribution:	11%

Sales & Royalty Summary Goal

	Year 1	Year 2		Comparison	
				Yr 1 Actual vs.	Yr 2 Budget vs.
	Actual	Budget	Estimate	Yr 2 Budget	Estimate
Sales	2,500,000	3,500,000	3,750,000	40%	7%
Royalites	250,000	350,000	375,000	40%	7%

Retailer Summary Goal

	Year 1		Year 2		
Retailer	Sales	Royalties	Sales	Royalties	% of Estimate
Walmart	658,000	65,800	770,000	77,000	21%
Target	475,000	47,500	573,000	57,300	15%
The Home Depot	378,000	37,800	425,000	42,500	11%
Lowe's	299,000	29,900	411,000	41,100	11%
SAM's Club	108,000	10,800	379,000	37,900	10%
Costco	107,000	10,700	368,000	36,800	10%
SEARS	97,000	9,700	320,000	32,000	9%
Kmart	75,000	7,500	144,000	14,400	4%
Kohl's	55,000	5,500	110,000	11,000	3%
Other	248,000	24,800	250,000	25,000	7%
Total	2,500,000	250,000	3,750,000	375,000	100%

Product Summary Goal

	Year 1		Year 2		
Product	Sales	Royalties	Sales	Royalties	% of Estimate
A	658,000	65,800	770,000	77,000	21%
B	475,000	47,500	573,000	57,300	15%
C	378,000	37,800	425,000	42,500	11%
D	299,000	29,900	411,000	41,100	11%
E	108,000	10,800	379,000	37,900	10%
F	107,000	10,700	368,000	36,800	10%
G	97,000	9,700	320,000	32,000	9%
H	75,000	7,500	144,000	14,400	4%
I	55,000	5,500	110,000	11,000	3%
J	248,000	24,800	250,000	25,000	7%
Total	2,500,000	250,000	3,750,000	375,000	100%

Figure 14-1: Annual Business Plan

FIGURE 2.7   Sample Licensee Business Plan

Case # 4 – Partnerships with Licensees – Disney and Mattel

Licensor: Disney
Licensee: Mattel
Term: Began in 1988 and ran to 2016; the license was relaunched in 2022

FIGURE 2.8   Disney Princess Merida
Source: Credit: iStock

Situation: Mattel, the company behind Barbie, first began in 1945 as a collaboration between Ruth and Elliot Handler, as well as Harold "Matt" Matson. Disney and Mattel's history dates back to 1955 when Mattel became the first year-round sponsor of the Mickey Mouse Club TV series (Time Staff Writer, 1962) at a cost of $500,000, equal to Mattel's net worth at the time. Up until this time, toy manufacturers relied primarily on retailers to show and sell their products and advertising occurred only during the holiday season; never before had a toy company spent money on advertising year-round. With television, however, toys could be marketed directly to children throughout the country. Thus, with the slogan, "You can tell it's Mattel, it's swell," the Handlers began a marketing revolution in the toy industry that produced an immediate payoff. As a result of the partnership, Mattel company sold many toy Burp Guns and made the Mattel brand name well-known among the viewing audience, dramatically driving their sales.

Task: Knowing the power of the Disney brand to sell Mattel toys through advertising, Mattel saw a benefit of licensing-in Disney characters to be sold in retail and at Disney theme parks.

Action: Mattel secured licensing rights from The Walt Disney Company for a new line of infant and preschool plush toys in 1988, to develop and sell toys at three Disney theme parks. Mattel also negotiated the exclusive rights to sell dolls, stuffed characters and preschool toys based on Disney characters. In 1993, Mattel was looking for a way to celebrate the 35th anniversary of Barbie and turned to Disney. The two created a stage show for Disney Parks, titled "The Magical World of Barbie." The show ran from 1993 to 1995 in EPCOT. Disney chose EPCOT to bolster its sales when there was a decline in attendance. The show premiered during the 1993 Thanksgiving season at the America Gardens Theater. The show featured Barbie, Ken and a cast of other characters, such as Skipper, Midge and Stacie. Through the use of props and vehicles, Barbie and her friends traveled around the world with various song and dance numbers.

Results: Based on Mattel's strong and enduring strategic alliance with The Walt Disney Company, Mattel gained the right to develop and sell toys at three Disney theme parks. Moreover, the agreement gave Mattel unparalleled exposure to millions of children and adults who visited the parks each year. Mattel also negotiated the exclusive rights to sell dolls, stuffed characters, and preschool toys based on Disney movie characters, such as those from Cinderella, Beauty and the Beast, and Aladdin. According to Mattel's company records, sales for the Disney line topped $500 million by 1995. Mattel earned the first grant for the Disney Princess doll license in 2000, along with rights to Disney characters such as Mickey and Minnie Mouse. Mattel added a princess-themed Barbie line in 2010. Its rights went until 2016. When Barbie sales began plummeting in 2012, Mattel lost the Disney license to Hasbro. In 2022, Mattel and Disney announced a multi-year global licensing agreement for Disney Princesses and Disney's Frozen, allowing Mattel to develop lines of toys on the properties. The latest collection of dolls was available for purchase in January 2023 (Verdon, 2022).

Case # 5 – Partnerships with Agents – Beanstalk and P&G

Licensor: P&G
Licensing Agency: Beanstalk
Term: 2007 to Present

P&G was founded in 1837 by two brothers-in-law making candles and soap. Today, P&G has grown into a global company with a long history of quality products and innovation that also boasts a thriving and exceptional trademark licensing program.

Situation: P&G began its first licensing agreement in the mid-1980s when its brand Vidal Sasoon extended a license to Conair, a best-in-class manufacturer of hair dryers. That license is still in effect today (2023). From that first license until the early 2000s, P&G's brand licensing program grew modestly, if not tactically. The company saw that it had the potential to substantially grow its brand licensing program while increasing the equity in its brands and driving royalty revenue to the company.

Task: P&G was interested in finding a strategic way to grow its brand licensing program to better connect its brands with consumers and drive royalty revenue.

Action: Looking to improve its results, P&G entered a relationship in 2007 with Beanstalk, a top brand licensing agency, where Beanstalk would represent P&G's family of brands to the industry. Through the help of Beanstalk, P&G takes care to nurture its licensing partnerships using market research to inform a thoroughly considered, data-driven approach to sustained success. For P&G, brand licensing has evolved into an integral part of its business strategy with corporate oversight from Global Business Development (License Global Staff, 2018).

Results: Going on 17 years as of the printing of this book, the relationship between Beanstalk and P&G is one of the longest-standing agency partnerships in the field of brand licensing and consumer products. P&G holds the position as a gold standard in corporate brand licensing, and in 2019 it was ranked No. 17 on License Global's ranking of the Top 150 Global Licensors, with $3.5 billion in license product sales. This coveted annual list ranks and recognizes licensors who lead the pack in retail licensed product sales each year. The Beanstalk Group is the world's leading brand licensing consultancy. Beanstalk helps its clients license their famous trademarks, copyrights and images to enhance the value of their brands and to create new revenue streams.

Case # 6 – Hasbro and Panini Partner with NBPA to Create Innovative Monopoly Game

Hasbro and Panini America came together with the NBA and NBA Players Association to create a new Monopoly board game that uses NBA Prizm Trading Cards.

Licensor: NBA and National Basketball Players Association (NBPA)
Licensees: Hasbro and Panini
Licensed Properties: NBA and NBA Players Names, Identities, Likenesses (NILs) and Monopoly
Category: Board Games and Trading Cards
Retail Partners: Available exclusively at Target from April 16 – July 31, 2023 and other major retailers beginning August 1, 2023
Territory: North America
Situation: Hasbro, a global branded entertainment leader whose mission is to entertain and connect generations of fans through storytelling and play, has targeted the segment of people who loved playing Monopoly and also loved card collecting. Monopoly is one of the world's favorite family game brands and is enjoyed by more than 1 billion players in 114 countries across the globe. Fans can engage with the Monopoly brand across many platforms and formats including live events, fashion licensing, digital gaming, casino gambling and more. The team, guided by their purpose to create joy and community for all people around the world, through a game, a toy, a story at a time, realized there was a unique opportunity to combine the activities of playing Monopoly and card collecting by bringing an

innovative trading card element to the game of Monopoly. The key for their success was to find the right partner and property to make the idea come to life. The Hasbro team knew that Panini America, a subsidiary of The Panini Group, was a significant publisher of sports trading cards and collectibles in the US, and held official licenses for NASCAR, NFL, NFLPA, NBA, NBPA, FIFA, UFC, WWE, College, Disney and other key properties.

Task: For Hasbro: Use the insights that the research team gleaned and their Monopoly board game and convince Panini America to partner with them to create a unique and compelling new product. For Panini America: leverage their existing assets and distribution channels to grow their business wherever possible.

Action: Hasbro Gaming, a division of Hasbro, partnered with Panini to create a new Monopoly edition called Monopoly Prizm. In 2009, Panini America signed a licensing agreement with the NBA and NBPA to become their exclusive trading card partner. Panini America, aware that the NBPA was dedicated to uncovering shared interests between their players and leading brands to build more engaging partnerships, believed they would be interested in the opportunity. The National Basketball Players Association is the union for current professional basketball players in the National Basketball Association (NBA). Established in 1954, the NBPA's mission is to protect and support the rights and talents of their players, magnify the power of their collective will, and amplify their voices as leaders who will transcend sport and society globally. Utilizing Panini's rights, Hasbro and Panini America were able to incorporate authentic trading cards, real player statistics and collectible card packs to expand the game, bringing the NBA court to the Monopoly board. In this Panini NBA trading card version of the Monopoly board game, players compete and earn points by revealing the NBA Player Ratings and Stats on the backs of their Panini cards. First, they'll use the Panini cards to draft their own team of four NBA players. Then, instead of buying properties in traditional Monopoly rules, players try to take control of NBA Games and collect bonus points when opponents land on them. To earn more points, players compare the stats on their Panini cards when they compete in Playmaker challenges and All-Star Contests. They can also use the Panini cards to trade NBA players or draft new ones. At the end of the game, the player with the most points wins.

Results: As a continuing evolution of the gaming industry, Hasbro and Panini America, through a collaboration with the NBA and NBPA, found a new way to celebrate the game of basketball.

After nearly two years of development and collaboration, Monopoly Prizm: NBA Edition board game launched on April 16, 2023, as a direct response to the excitement and interest of NBA fans. Prizm, the most popular global NBA trading card brand from Panini America, anchors the Monopoly Prizm: NBA Edition board game and features a 90-card base set.

Noteworthy: The global popularity of the Prizm trading card brand matched perfectly with the Monopoly brand to introduce an NBA trading cardboard game. It captures all the elements of Monopoly while introducing "special parallels and rare inserts" to enhance gameplay that has made NBA trading cards popular and collectible. Monopoly Prizm: NBA Edition showcases NBA players building their collective influence globally, an important goal of the NBPA (Licensing International Staff, 2023).

Case #7 – 2010 FIFA World Cup Championships in South Africa – FIFA and the Master Licensee Agreement with Licensing Matters Global

This case considers a global brand that offers a variety of products licensed. It shows how products and companies work in harmony to support the brand promise in Sport, Video Games, Entertainment and Edutainment, that is, entertainment with an educational aspect. The case is focused on FIFA World Cup Championships in South Africa which took place in 2010 to emphasize the double side of licensing. It is based on an interview with the owner of Licensing Matters Global in the year 2016.

Situation: In 2005 FIFA was needed to maximize its licensing rights for the 2010 FIFA World Cup quadrennial whose men's championships were held in South Africa. Licensing the FIFA marks is a major component of the execution of any World Cup program.

Task: FIFA needed to find a qualified Master Licensee who could manage the program on their behalf and achieve their business objectives. This license included the copyrights, the trademark and the wordmark for FIFA back to the time of its founding, 1904.

Action: FIFA signed a Master Licensee Agreement with Licensing Matters Global. According to Mark Matheny, LMG, who with several business partners acquired the master license from FIFA in early 2006 for the 2010 FIFA World Cup quadrennial, FIFA required that the Master Licensing Agreement minimum financial guarantee be paid using cash or secured by a Letter of Credit and/or Bank Guarantee. FIFA uses guarantees of this type to finance their operational costs related to its competitions, such as the World Cup and all their other World Championships, for which a worldwide license was acquired. LMG, as the Master Licensee, had rights to create merchandise for clothing, sporting goods, collectibles, souvenirs and a host of other categories. Licensing Matters Global goal was to maximize the rights to the FIFA brand in every category globally and to drive royalty revenue to cover the minimum guaranteed royalties. LMG created a FIFA football retail concept, which included the products of the trademark, and copyrights acquired plus those of other companies, creating a unique and authentic football-themed shopping experience. LMG also developed a concept based on FIFA's event-based business – where 70 percent of the licensing revenue typically came from the host nation – and made it a global platform. Considering the size of the Minimum Guarantee, which was significant, LMG had to activate in multiple countries to make the program financially successful. LMG hired a merchandising team to develop a detailed digital toolkit that covered everything. The toolkit was sent to manufacturing partners to replicate the designs on products in a way to adjust for seasonality – northern and southern hemispheres and local tastes. With FIFA's approval, LMG created an Official Event Retailer concept. By becoming an Official Event Retailer, it was allowed to bring people in-store to buy officially licensed products and other products marketed by FIFA's partnership network, such as Electronic Arts FIFA game, Panini football cards and even football-themed Coca-Cola licensed merchandise. Moreover, LMG gave the consumer a chance to win an all-expense paid trip to go to the FIFA World Cup in South Africa.

Results: LMG ended up activating the rights in over 60 countries with official retailers all over the world – from the UK to US, and from Indonesia to Brazil. Walmart was a partner in 14 countries. By incorporating the retailer into the program, LMG stripped out the time required to manage a licensee network. LMG ended up placing official licensed FIFA product in 5,000 store locations with 1 million square feet of retail selling space.

Noteworthy: The main reasons for the success of this extension are the FIFA brand's potential to expand into new markets and categories, and consequently a strong connection between the brand's core products and the categories in which it was licensed, favorable licensing agreement terms to meet both parties' business objectives over the long term, generating high financial outcomes, for example, strong sales or profit, and the commitment toward the partnership both from the licensor and the licensee.

References

Aitken, M., Baskaran, S., Lamarre, E., Silber, M., & Waters, S. (2000). A license to cure. *The McKinsey Quarterly*, (1), 80.

Aloosh, A., Aloosh, M., Tarighati, T., & Baghini, H. S. (2006, June). Extended products banding issues. In *2006 IEEE International Technology Management Conference (ICE)* (pp. 1–8). IEEE.

Batra, R., Lenk, P., & Wedel, M. (2010). Brand extension strategy planning: Empirical estimation of brand – Category personality fit and atypicality. *Journal of Marketing Research*, 47(2), 335–347.

Battersby, G. (2019). *Licensing royalty rates*, 2020 ed. Wolters Kluwer.

Belu, M., & Caragin, A. R. (2008). Strategies of entering new markets. *The Romanian Economic Journal*, 27(1), 83–98.

Canalichio, P. (2018). *Expand, grow, thrive: 5 Proven steps to turn good brands into global brands through the LASSO method*. Emerald Publishing Limited.

Canalichio, P. (2019). *Grow brand value while accelerating revenue growth*. Entrepreneur Media.

Cardinali, S., Travaglini, M., & Giovannetti, M. (2019). Increasing brand orientation and brand capabilities using licensing: An opportunity for SMES in international markets. *Journal of the Knowledge Economy*, 10, 1808–1830.

Chernev, A. (2020). *Strategic brand management*. Cerebellum Press.

Chesbrough, H. (2006). *Open business models: How to thrive in the new innovation landscape*. Harvard Business Press.

Cooper, J. (2023). *Intellectual property piracy in the time of the metaverse*. The Law Review of the Franklin Pierce Center for IP. https://law.unh.edu/blog/2023/06/idea-volume-63-number-3

Cross, B. (2015). The effective use of licensing in brand strategy. *Journal of Brand Strategy*, 4(4), 357–362.

Eisenmann, T. R. (2008). Managing proprietary and shared platforms. *California Management Review*, 50(4), 31–53.

Frey, C. B., Ansar, A., & Wunsch-Vincent, S. (2015). Defining and measuring the "market for brands": Are emerging economies catching up? *The Journal of World Intellectual Property*, 18(5), 217–244.

Goldscheider, R. (Ed.). (2002). *Licensing best practices: The LESI guide to strategic issues and contemporary realities*. John Wiley & Sons.

Goldscheider, R., & Gordon, A. (2006). *Licensing best practices: Strategic, territorial and technology issues*. John Wiley & Sons.

Guyot, O. (2017). Canali inks eyewear deal with L'amy America. *Fashion Network*. www.fashion-network.com/news/Canali-inks-eyewear-deal-with-l-amy-america,869625.html

Hirt, M., & Willmott, P. (2014). Strategic principles for competing in the digital age. *McKinsey Quarterly*, 5(1), 1–13.

Hitt, M. A., King, D. R., Krishnan, H., Makri, M., Schijven, M., Shimizu, K., & Zhu, H. (2012). *Creating value through mergers and acquisitions: Challenges and opportunities*. Marquette University.

Jayachandran, S., Kaufman, P., Kumar, V., & Hewett, K. (2013). Brand licensing: What drives royalty rates? *Journal of Marketing, 77*(5), 108–122.

Lewis, J. D. (2002). *Partnerships for profit: Structuring and managing strategic alliances.* Simon and Schuster.

License Global Staff Writer. (2018). *Procter & gamble: Leader of the brands.* License Global.

Licensing International Staff. (2023). *Hasbro and Panini America partner to bring NBA Prizm trading cards to monopoly in a new board game.* Licensing International.

Lotman, J. (2020). *Invisible marketing: A hidden tool for connecting with consumers through licensing.* Lioncrest Publishing.

Mottner, S., & Johnson, J. P. (2000). Motivations and risks in international licensing: A review and implications for licensing to transitional and emerging economies. *Journal of World Business, 35*(2), 171–188.

Muhonen, T., Hirvonen, S., & Laukkanen, T. (2017). SME brand identity: Its components, and performance effects. *Journal of Product & Brand Management, 26*(1), 52–67.

Odoom, R., Agbemabiese, G. C., Anning-Dorson, T., & Mensah, P. (2017). Branding capabilities and SME performance in an emerging market: The moderating effect of brand regulations. *Marketing Intelligence & Planning, 35*(4), 473–487.

Parr, R. (2007). *Royalty rates for licensing intellectual property.* John Wiley & Sons.

Perrier, R. (1998). Brand licensing. In *Brands: The new wealth creators* (pp. 104–113). Palgrave Macmillan.

Petromilli, M., Morrison, D., & Million, M. (2002). Brand architecture: Building brand portfolio value. *Strategy & Leadership, 30*(5), 22–28.

Portee, A. (2020). Outdoor wear and luxury fashion team up with the north face and Gucci collaborating in the spirit of exploration. *Forbes.* www.forbes.com/sites/allysonportee/2020/12/22/outdoor-wear-and-luxury-fashion-team-up-with-the-north-face-and-gucci-collaborating-in-the-spirit-of-exploration/?sh=391fc1dc1932

Prajit, G. (2023). *Protecting intellectual property in the metaverse: Challenges, opportunities, and recent case laws, voices, tech.* TOI.

Raugust, K. (2004). *The licensing business handbook.* EPM Communications.

Reese, H. (2011). *How to license your million dollar idea: Cash in on your inventions, new product ideas, software, web business ideas, and more.* John Wiley & Sons.

Reyes, M. (2017). *Luxottica, tiffany renew license agreement. Market intelligence.* S&P Global.

Richardson, J. H. (2014). The Spotify paradox: How the creation of a compulsory license scheme for streaming on-demand music platforms can save the music industry. *UCLA Entertainment Law Review, 22,* 45.

Robinson, A. B., Tuli, K. R., & Kohli, A. K. (2015). Does brand licensing increase a licensor's shareholder value. *Management Science, 61*(6), 1436–1455.

Sałamacha, A. (2020). Building brand protection strategy in contemporary enterprises. *Research Papers of Wroclaw University of Economics and Business, 64*(12), 87–100.

Santo, A. (2015). *Selling the silver bullet: The lone ranger and transmedia brand licensing.* University of Texas Press.

Seavy, M. (2023). *Flavors from the bar to the grill: Fireball™, Buffalo Trace™ and Southern Comfort™-inspired seasonings set to launch this month.* Licensing international.

Sherman, A. J. (1991). *Franchising and licensing: Two ways to build your business.* AMACON: American Marketing Association.

Siegel, D. S., & Wright, M. (2015). University technology transfer offices, licensing, and start-ups. *Chicago Handbook of University Technology Transfer and Academic Entrepreneurship, 1*(40), 84–103.

Simon, D., & Battersby, G. J. (2011). *Basics of licensing: How to extend brand and entertainment properties for profit.* Kent Press.

Staff. (1962). Corporations: All's swell at Mattel. *Time Magazine.* https://content.time.com/time/subscriber/article/0,33009,874558,00.html

Stone, M. (2018). *The power of licensing: Harnessing brand equity.* American Bar Association.

Stone, M., & Trebbien, J. D. (2019). Brand licensing: A powerful marketing tool for today's shopping battlefield. *Journal of Brand Strategy, 8*(3), 207–217.

Travaglini, M., Cardinali, S., & Gregori, G. L. (2015, June). Creating a brand strategy for SMES using licensing: An exploratory analysis in footwear industry. In *2015 Global Fashion Management*

Conference at Florence (pp. 245–263). www.researchgate.net/publication/279224363_CREATING_A_BRAND_STRATEGY_FOR_SMEs_USING_LICENSING_AN_EXPLORA-TORY_ANALYSIS_IN_FOOTWEAR_INDUSTRY

Verdon, J. (2022). Mattel convinces Disney it will love the princesses better than Hasbro. *Forbes.* www.forbes.com/sites/joanverdon/2022/01/26/mattel-convinces-disney-it-will-love-the-princesses-better-than-hasbro/?sh=529584a58e3e

Verma, R., & Kumar, M. (2022). Brand extension in FMCG sector through social media enabled CRM and investigating its impact on brand equity. In *Building a brand image through electronic customer relationship management* (pp. 201–236). IGI Global.

Völckner, F., & Sattler, H. (2006). Drivers of brand extension success. *Journal of Marketing, 70*(2), 18–34.

Weszka, P. (2014). *Leverage of a sport mega-event branding: A case study of the 2010 FIFA world cup.* University of Johannesburg.

Wiedmann, K. P., & Ludewig, D. (2008). How risky are brand licensing strategies in view of customer perceptions and reactions? *Journal of General Management, 33*(3), 31–52.

3
DESIGNING AN ENDURING-BASED LICENSING PROGRAM

Learning Objectives

The aim of the chapter is to provide content and tools to answer the following questions: How important is brand positioning in designing enduring licensing programs? What are the attributes that define a brand architecture, making it distinctive and valuable? What are the growth directions of the brand that allow hidden brand value to be unlocked? After reading this chapter, readers will be able to fully understand the centrality of the brand positioning and the brand value in itself for building a successful and enduring licensing program. They will be able to identify the brand positioning sets and the attributes comprising its architecture, and analyze the points of parity and points of difference. Readers will learn to craft a brand positioning statement, combining the three dimensions, target market, unique value, reasons to believe, in an original way. They also will be able to evaluate where and how a brand can grow, through a strategy of brand expansion, brand extension and/or internationalization. Finally, they will be able to select appropriate tools and evaluate critically what brands are ready to be licensed.

Keywords: Brand Positioning, Brand Architecture, Points of Pair, Points of Difference, Brand Value, Brand Extension, Brand Expansion, Brand Internationalization, Brand License-ability.

1. The Centrality of Brand Positioning in Enduring Licensing Programs

To fully understand the strategic value of licensing both for the licensor and for the licensee, it is important to analyze the issues related to the centrality of the brand positioning and the brand value in itself.

A brand is a name, term, sign, symbol or combination of these, which identifies the maker or seller of the product or service (Kotler & Armstrong, 2017; Keller & Swaminathan, 2019; Maurya & Mishra, 2012). Brands are redefined as complex multidimensional constructs with varying degrees of meaning, independence, co-creation and scope. Brands are semiotic marketing systems that generate value for direct and indirect participants, society

DOI: 10.4324/9781003364566-4

and the broader environment, through the exchange of co-created meaning (Conejo & Wooliscroft, 2015). The brand affixed to the product helps the consumer understand where it was manufactured or produced. A brand owner distinguishes the products or services from other brand's competition. Consumers, in turn, can be assured the product they are purchasing is exactly what they want. Wong and Merrilees (2008) analyze barriers to branding and the performance benefits of being brand oriented. For others, a good brand reputation gives customers an idea of what to expect from the company. Based on its reputation, a brand will convey a level of quality, reliability and durability. The relationship with consumers starts when the brand fully represents the needs of its target audience while also making sure that they are continually delivering on a promise they've made. Once the relationship with the brand is developed, consumers make their purchases based on the commitments the brand makes, the consistency of these commitments, and the way they make consumers feel (Halloran, 2014). Brands also lead consumers to develop certain expectations of products. The longer consumers experience predictable quality and consistent performance, the more they will grow to expect any new products sold under the same brand to have the same qualities and attributes (Martinez, 2022). Consider Gucci, Lamborghini and Rolex brands, which are examples of successful brands. Consumers are exposed to them through a variety of outlets such as in-store and online retailers, mass commercial broadcasts or magazines. Each brand has its own products, services and expectations that differentiate it from its competitors. Gucci has built a reputation and level of addictiveness that has caused customers to fall in love with the brand. Lamborghini goes beyond high-performance automobiles and gets closer to roads, highlighting. They say, "We are not supercars. We are Lamborghini. Follow your ears." This speaks to the brand's sense of harmony with the driver and the road. Rolex has been ranked number one for global reputation and top consumer super brands. It stands for quality, style, reliability and distinction.

A brand can sometimes be represented by a person. If he/she can identify what he/she stands for and communicate that promise with his/her audience on a personal level that evokes feelings. Michael Jordan, a six-time NBA champion, is a branding juggernaut. Jordan made License Global's 2019 Influentials list, honoring the licensing industry's paradigm-shifting disruptors. Dubbed "The World's Richest Athlete" by Forbes, Jordan is destroying the competition in footwear. Nike's Jordan brand brought in $3.14 billion in revenue in the fiscal year ending May 2019. In 2019, Jordan himself earned an estimated $145 million, according to Forbes, which also estimated last year that the star's cumulative off-court income since entering the NBA in 1984 was roughly $1.7 billion (Wardak, 2020) Consider Catherine Elizabeth Middleton, Princess of Galles and wife of Prince William. She's well-known for wearing inexpensive outfits versus wearing expensive fashion brands. She wants to demonstrate that a simple look is always the right choice during certain featured events (Mackelden, 2018). Since Princess Kate's marriage to Prince William, each brand of clothing she wears is intensively reviewed by publications around the globe. This worldwide coverage has sparked tremendous interest in the "Princess Kate" brand. Many brands that she has worn thus far, including the shoe brand, Aquazzura, have experienced a boost in sales and an increase in global recognition (Royce, 2023). The key to this success is that Princess Kate has chosen brands that coincide with her positioning in society. Princess Kate is not followed by the media and her followers just because she married Prince William but because she has become a style icon. She formed strong bonds with her fans, who expect more and more from her. She has not entered categories that disrupt the relationships she has already developed. In a sense, the "Princess Kate" brand has become attractive and engaging, allowing relationships themselves to be managed proactively to keep customers constantly looking out for new opportunities to engage.

Brand positioning is central to build a successful and enduring brand licensing program. As brand owner, it is critical to understand a brand's positioning in order to avoid miscommunication between the brand and the consumer. If this happens, the consumer will have a misperception of the brand and be confused about the brand's position in the marketplace. As a licensee, it's critical to understand the brand positioning of the licensor. It is vital to licensing that a brand owner develops a clear understanding of a potential brand positioning beforehand. The unintended consequences of a wrong positioning could create confusion in the marketplace and make the licensee's job much more difficult. US supermodel Kendall Jenner has signed a deal with Adidas as an Adidas Original Ambassador. Since she represents a "brand" herself, it is profitable for her to use licensing in order to grow her brand. With respect to Adidas' positioning, Kendall is associated with an athletic brand although she is a non-athlete. Kendall is fit, young, vibrant and represents a target of the market that Adidas is unable to reach. Many people today who wear Adidas do not consider themselves athletes. So, signing with Jenner may encourage non-athletic consumers to purchase the Adidas brand for daily wear, fashion and athletic purposes. For the brand owner, the question this choice raises is how successful the Adidas brand will be with Kendall Jenner. For the licensee, the question is, "how this partnership can reinforce Kendall's brand positioning in the marketplace?"

Brand positioning defines the target market, their need, how the brand satisfies that need and how the brand differentiates itself from the competition. Brand Positioning sets the foundation for how the brand's function and emotional benefits are communicated, making it critical to the success of brand licensing. Specifically, brand positioning refers to designing the offering and brand image to occupy a distinct place in the mind of the target market (Keller, 2019). Getting a brand into the mind of the target market allows them to think about the brand when they think about a product or a service that solves a problem they have. The objective of positioning is to reach out and be in and on the minds of the stakeholders, so they think about the brand when they need a product, the suppliers so as to connect the brand with someone else in the supply network; customers so as to retain them, and prospects so that they'll consider a brand. Positioning connects the brand with its advocates. According to Forbes, the 2022 top ten brands in the world based on brand value are Apple ($241B), Google ($207B), Microsoft ($163B), Amazon ($135B), Facebook ($70B), Coca-Cola ($64B), Disney ($61B), Samsung ($50B), Louis Vuitton ($47B) and McDonalds ($46B). Reflecting on the top three brands, no one is doing better than Apple, which is leading the pack at No. 1 in the world and No. 1 in market value for the company. Google is also doing well, due to top-of-mind awareness when an Internet search needs to be done. Google is much more than that; it's on mobile devices and electronic vehicles: it's a way to analyze the website, it's an email platform, and it has ventured into artificial intelligence (AI). All of which has resulted in Google becoming the No. 2 brand in the world. With the consistent changes and new innovative ways Google has created for users, Google is constantly adding value to the brand, making the brand what it is today. The No. 3 spot is claimed by Microsoft, which is an American technology company that operates on a multinational platform. Microsoft has been around for decades, but they still are finding new and creative ways to reinvent themselves to add more value to the brand. Microsoft is phenomenally successful and probably will continue to be for decades further. Besides investing in brand reputation, these brands expand their businesses through licensing strategy according to License Global as reported in their Leading 2022 Licensees Report.

Identifying the brand positioning sets the foundation for building a licensing program, making the brand positioning critical to the success of brand licensing as well.

2. Brand Positioning Statement, Brand Architecture and Points of Difference

The brand positioning statement expresses in a unified way three dimensions of the corporate strategy, which are mission, purpose and vision. Mission indicates "how" to achieve a medium to long-term business goal. Purpose is "why," explaining why a company begins and undertakes a path. The vision is "what": it describes what a company will be like if it has achieved its mission.

Beliefs and values inspire the mission statement and are the foundation of why a company exists.

Beliefs are assumptions held to be true and may or may not be based on facts. Beliefs can be rigid, causing divisions, and range from general topics to deeper, more specific topics. Values motivate actions, govern the way to interact with others and help make decisions. They are universal concepts, which bring people together, and also mature through experience. Values affect moral, behavior and character. They can include concepts like fairness, justice, freedom and equality. The personality traits express the origins, history and way in which a company presents itself to the market and what kind of experience customers can have. It is communicated through images, symbols and even customer service policies.

Brand architecture ensures a brand is properly organized to support its position. Beliefs and values drive the brand architecture, which consists of physical attributes, functional benefits, a core message, emotional benefits and a brand promise. A company uses its story and architecture to write a brand positioning statement (Adıgüzel, 2020).

The next step for developing brand architecture is to identify and establish points of parity and points of difference to establish the right identity and brand image. Points of parity are the minimum attributes that are expected by the target and prospective customers. If the firm does not meet that minimum, the offer is not viable. Points of difference are the attributes that really stand out and differentiate from the competition. While the points of parity keep a brand in good stead, the points of difference make it excellent and unique.

Positioning basically says there's a problem out there that a company promises to fix for a specific target audience, and then it substantiates why that company is the best to fix that problem. In the positioning, a company explains how its solution differs from the competition and provides an authoritative metric to reinforce why a company can make that claim (Keller & Brexendorf, 2019). The company uses its story and architecture to write its brand position to distinguish itself from peers; the architecture will align with the company, what it brings, and will ensure the positioning is distinct and on solid ground (Hsu et al., 2016). The positioning statement contains the following key points:

- *Target Market.* What are the types of businesses or who are the types of consumers you want to reach? What are their interests? How do they make decisions? What influences them and why? The more specific the answers are, the better success to have in fulfilling needs at a very high level. The description should be based on demographics, psychographics and values.
- *Unique Value.* What do you provide to the target audience? Do you think you're the best in your category? What's the genius statement for your product or company? What do you do? What value do you provide your customers that no one else can provide?

- *Reasons to Believe.* How can a company back up its statements? This can mean anything from showing the process to sharing data statements to prove that it is for real. Make a list of the reasons to believe. The more proof points a company can provide, the better. Finally, three questions can plugged into the brand positioning statement, as follows:

> *[Brand Name] provides (Target Market) with (Unique Value) than any other [Company Industry]. The Company does this by (Reason to Believe 1), (Reason to Believe 2), and (Reason to Believe 3).*

The Rubbermaid brand positioning statement is a clear example of brand positioning, no matter the country. Rubbermaid is a 70-plus-year-old American icon. The Rubbermaid brand positioning statement targets the self-assured balancers, who are independent, proactive women ages 18–54 who, in seeking to balance their lives, put so much into their day they need to replenish what's been taken out (Target Market). The point of difference consists in providing ingeniously durable ways to personalize the environment so as to feel empowered (Unique Value). The reasons to believe are related to the use of high-quality materials to ensure long-lasting products designed to get the job done easily and quickly every time.

CHECKLIST FOR A BRAND POSITIONING STATEMENT

Table 3.1 lists the essential elements and distinctive attributes that make up a brand's architecture. From their combination it is possible to identify the points of parity and difference with respect to competitors and the answers to the three questions (Target Market, Unique Value and Reasons to Believe) that make up the brand positioning statement.

TABLE 3.1 Checklist for a Brand Positioning Statement

Purpose, Mission and Vision	Why, What and How	Brand Architecture
Brand distinctive traits	Why brand exists	Brand main characteristics
Brand purpose	Why brand do what it does	What the brand stands for
Brand vision	What brand does	Five words describing the brand
Brand mission	How brand does it	Brand physical attributes
Brand core beliefs	Why anyone would work for this brand	Brand functional advantages
Brand core values	Why anyone would buy this brand	Brand core message
	Why anyone should be interested in this brand	Brand emotional benefits
		Brand promise
Points of parity	....	
	....	
Points of difference	....	
	....	

(Continued)

Purpose, Mission and Vision	Why, What and How	Brand Architecture

TABLE 3.1 (Continued)

- **Target Market** ....
- **Unique Value** ....
- **Reasons to Believe**

Reason 1 ....
Reason 2 ....
Reason 3 ....

3. Brand Growth to Unlock Licensing Latent Value

Brand licensing is more than a commercial sales strategy used to access the licensor's distribution network for the purpose of increasing sales and entering new markets. Brand licensing is a growth strategy. Companies adopt licensing with a brand portfolio-building approach, trying to exploit the propensity of consumers toward the positive values associated with brand images for the products that make up their core business (Reid et al., 2005). Firms look at brand licensing strategically as they seek to integrate their own and licensed brand portfolios to overcome brand barriers. Finally, brand licensings support the development of a proprietary brand as they signal the licensee's brand orientation (Chadwick & Holt, 2008).

Brand growth indicates the expansion/development of a brand in terms of quantitative (more use) or qualitative (better use), having the purpose, respectively, of conquering a new and different market position or achieving a higher level of revenues or market shares. Brand growth is also when a brand expands the core business into a new geographic region or further saturates an existing region. It continues the business where the brand is already in, offering more of the same to new audiences in different locales. The brand growth concerns both mono-brand companies and multi-brand ones, both small- and medium-sized companies and large companies (Martinez, 2022). Of strategic importance are the questions relating to the growth directions and tools through brand licensing since they concern the choices of where and how to expand.

Growth Directions (Where?): Brand extension, brand expansion and brand internationalization are three directions of growth. They continue the business the brand is already in, offering more of the same to new audiences in different locales. *Brand extension*, known as line extension, is about building out a brand product portfolio. It's about a brand continuation in the current portfolio, having the goal to force the market or to win over competitors' customers. *Brand expansion*, also known as category extension, is perceived as more risky than brand extension. Brands broaden their presence into markets where they have not built their reputation, and, often, they rely on licensees to fill the experience and capacity gap on their behalf. In addition to the possibility of entering sectors traditionally not covered by the licensor, brand expansion can be adopted as a strategy to modernize the brand or to enter markets where there are legal restrictions that require the presence of local partners for the sale of foreign products. *Brand internationalization* indicates that growth, in terms of brand extension and brand expansion, may occur in a new geographical region or may further saturate an existing region. Several factors influence the brand growth direction. They refer to the firm's resources, such as financial, human, technological, operational and intangible resources, to the entrepreneur's objectives and strategic capabilities, and to managerial skills, coordination and governance.

Growth Tools (How?): The growth, in terms of brand extension and brand expansion, can occur internally, externally through independent activity or mergers and acquisitions, or through collaborative agreements with or without risk capital participation. A franchising model is an option. When a company looks to grow by expanding its brands, it does so by taking the brand beyond its current confines – into areas where it hasn't been before. So, when companies talk about brand growth what they are really talking about is expanding an idea/thing/celebrity and/or object further into the lives of consumers. The mechanisms may vary but it is not just the brand itself, or its intellectual property, that is being leveraged. It is the relationships that people have with the brand because of how it appears, what it means to them and a desire to lift their involvement. The choice of licensee depends on the brand development stage: if the brand is in the product stage, the licensor is looking for a licensee to develop the main product category, while if it is in the warranty stage, a specialist or single category manufacturer is sought to make line extensions. If the brand is in its growth phase, the licensor is interested in business-specific licensees who can support the brand extension process on unrelated businesses.

BRAND GROWTH – 2023 FIFA WOMEN'S WORLD CUP

This case fits into the following areas: growth (primarily), expansion (FIFA, national teams and players) and internationalization.

Founded in 1904 to provide unity among national soccer associations, the Federation Internationale de Football Association (FIFA) boasts 209 members, rivaling that of the United Nations. As teams prepare for the upcoming 2023 FIFA Women's World Cup, each team is working to score big with licensing. The strategy has been building gradually for the past few years as teams take on licensing agencies – OneTeam Partners represents the US Women's National Soccer Team (USWNT), for example – and players launch businesses of their own. The USWNT received $1 million in royalty payments in 2019. This came after the US Soccer Federation settled an equity pay dispute with the women's team last year. "The USWNT's royalty rates are equal to, and in some cases, above [licensing] industry norms and higher for the 2023 World Cup than in 2019," said the SVP and Head of Consumer Products Licensing at OneTeam. The team will also field co-branded products with the soccer federation.

Although team and player jerseys remain the top sellers, the month-long World Cup featured a broader array of licensed products when it got underway on July 20, 2023, in Australia and New Zealand. The US Women's National Team (USWNT's) roster of licensees has grown to 38, including 16 new companies. That's a long way from the single licensee (Electronic Arts for the FIFA video game title) the USWNT had in 2017. The USWNT also expanded its licensing business into 3.75-inch action figures (Super7), limited-edition bobbleheads (Foco), mobile games (Matchday) and silver coins (Highland Mint). Nike will produce name and number children's tee shirts for the first time, while Legends operates USWNT's e-Commerce and in-venue stores for both USWNT and FIFA.

Meanwhile, the UK Women's National Team (the Lionesses) has netted millions of pounds in brand sponsorships. Fanatics ran retail operations during the Union of European Football Associations (UEFA) championships last year. Sales of merchandise have grown 150 percent since 2018, said Matthew Primack, SVP International Business Affairs and Development at Fanatics (Licensing International Staff, 2023). The array of licensees has gained a higher commitment from retailers. In the US, Dick's Sporting Goods, a retailer known for limiting sales to 40 stores offering a broad assortment of soccer-related goods, will carry USWNT team jerseys chainwide starting in July 2023. Target will merchandise jerseys in its sports department and offer Panini and Parkside trading cards near checkout, while Icon E-Com will handle print-on-demand. There are also player-owned e-Commerce businesses, including Beat Everybody (Allie Long, Alex Morgan and Kelley O'Hara) and Re-Inc (Tobin Heath, Meghan Kingenberg, Christen Press and Megan Rapinoe). The US team's success in merchandise will be influenced by the results. With the USWNT failing to make the knockout rounds, the officially licensed product may not last until 2024, when promotions for the Olympic Games in France will start.

BRAND EXTENSION – FERRARI LUXURY GOODS

Ferrari is a famous Italian luxury sports car manufacturer, based in Maranello (Italy). In addition to producing racing cars, Ferrari also produces sedans and sports cars for the luxury car market. The Ferrari brand licensing program is quite extensive (Vanamee, 2021). Several licensed products, including model cars, tee shirts, jackets, caps, sunglasses, perfumes, pins, umbrellas, suitcases, wallets and racing car kits, have the Ferrari brand. The miniature models of the pilots in red overalls have become icons and cult objects for fans and enthusiasts. However, the consumer market often does not perceive the connection between the sports car, the speed and adrenaline of Ferrari cars and licensed products, even if they are high-end and premium. Ferrari's brand extension strategy has not achieved the expected level of success.

From 2019, Ferrari has reduced the number of licensed products by around 50 percent, eliminating those that are not consistent with the corporate brand. Over the past two years, Ferrari has entered the luxury fashion market in line with the essence of this brand. In 2021 the company launched the first men's/women's/children's clothing collection signed by the stylist Rocco Iannone and opened a restaurant with a starred chef to offer a luxury gastronomic experience in line with the value of the Ferrari brand. The goal of Ferrari's repositioning was to transform the licensed brand into a lifestyle brand, which goes beyond motor sport (Deeny, 2021).

LICENSING AND BRAND EXPANSION OF ITALIAN FASHION

Licensing represents the strategy favored by companies in the fashion sector to encourage brand expansion in foreign markets and related businesses. The "global style project" is used to describe the potential of licensing to expand the creativity of fashion houses over a wide range of actions.

Brand licensing is used both by high fashion houses and by emerging stylists who, in agreement with the companies of the textile industry and with commercial partners, distribute the investments between the creativity of the Maison, the production of clothing and the selling of accessories and services connected to them to economically exploit the brand value. In particular, brand extension is the privileged strategy used for the expansion of the fashion brand owner in related business lines but of which the company does not possess skills and experience (Pozzo & Jacometti, 2016). Thus, for example, the design of footwear or the production of eyeglasses and sunglasses requires specific equipment and skills in terms of anatomy, optics and new materials that fashion houses often do not possess.

The diffusion of licensing took place around the 1960s by the French Maisons led by stylists such as Pierre Cardin, Coco Chanel, Yves Saint Laurent, Christian Dior, Louis Feraud, Guy La Roche and Jean Louis Scherrer. Chanel had granted the use of the brand for the Chanel N. 5 perfume, while Dior had licensed its brand for the production of hosiery to an American company. Pierre Cardin signed, for the first time in 1959, a licensing agreement with the French company Vaskene SA to produce women's clothing for a niche market.

In Italy, Giorgio Armani introduced a licensing model with the Gruppo Finanziario Tessile (GFT) in the late 1970s to produce a line of clothing bearing his name. The Armani agreement became a reference model for outlining the relationship between designer and manufacturing company on an equal footing. The designer contributed his creativity, while the Gruppo Finanziario Tessile ensured the continuity of production, its marketing and distribution. In the 1980s, licensing became the preferred tool for the expansion of the Armani brand on an industrial scale while the GFT held 60 licenses, becoming the Italian company with the largest number of licenses for brands production and distribution. In those years, several brands, including Valentino, Ungaro and Moschino, based their growth strategy on licensed production, in collaboration with clothing and service manufacturing companies. In the 1990s, the link between image and brand identity in the markets became a relevant strategic issue. The brand relationships between licensors and licensees were redefined. While the fashion houses (such as Armani) decided to participate financially in the licensee's activity, the production companies (such as the GFT) focused on the most important brands, reducing or eliminating the marginal lines.

BRAND INTERNATIONALIZATION – THE "SHARE A COKE" CAMPAIGN

Coke's research in Australia showed that while teens and young adults loved that Coca-Cola was big and iconic, many consumers felt the brand was not talking to them at eye level. Australians are egalitarian. There's a phrase in Australia called "tall poppy syndrome." It means that if anyone gets too big for their boots, they get cut down like a tall poppy. Lucie Austin, director of marketing for Coca-Cola South Pacific, challenged her agencies: "We need [you] to come back with something that makes everyone sit up because of its impact . . . and we only have a few weeks." The "Share a Coke" campaign was launched in 2011 in Australia (Codella, 2021). This campaign allowed consumers to purchase cans of Coke where the label is swapped out with popular first names. In the first summer, Coke sold more than 250 million named bottles and cans in a nation of just under 23 million people. Share a Coke was so popular that by 2015 more than 50 countries offered consumers the chance to buy cans with their favorite names on them. By 2016, Share a Coke was in 70 countries tapping into consumers' desires for personalization and customization.

4. Brand License-Ability

After analyzing how brand owners use licensing to expand their business and the first steps to ensure a best-in-class, built-to-last program, the next step is to understand what brands are ready to be licensed. A brand is license-able if it meets the following criteria (Keller & Swaminathan, 2019):

- It has high top-of-mind brand awareness when a category is mentioned, which means consumers name it when asked which brands are best in its class.
- The brand commands consumer loyalty and is therefore something that customers do not want to be without.
- Consumers understand the brand and embrace what it stands for. It achieves superior business results in its margin, sales growth and expandability.

Table 3.2 presents a scorecard that can help brand owners determine the license-ability of their brand. The scoring is not intended to be rigorous but rather to give the brand owner a sense for the relative strength of the brand with its target so as to ascertain the license-ability of the brand. When answering the questions in the table, each brand manager makes an educated guess at the answer and assigns an appropriate score. A score above 40 indicates the brand is a leader in at least four categories. If the score is below 40, the brand is not ready to be licensed. The true litmus test of license-ability is whether any company has any interest in securing a license in any category from the brand owner (Lotman, 2020). If no product or service provider has expressed an interest in licensing the brand, then the brand is not yet license-able.

TABLE 3.2 A Scorecard Table for Evaluating Brand License-ability

Criteria	Score 0–10 points for each criteria	Score Guide
High top-of-mind brand awareness with target audience	. . . . . ./10	For brands with an unaided top 3 ranking = 8–10 points; top 6 = 6–7 points top 10 = 4–5 points if aided = 1–3 points Otherwise = 0 points
Consumers who considered the brand as the best-in-class	. . . . . ./10	If yes = 10 points; if no = 0

Criteria	Score 0–10 points for each criteria	Score Guide
Consumers who do not want to be without the brand	. . . . . ./10	High number of advocates = 9–10 points Brand insisters = 7–8 points Loyalists = 5–6 points Consumers who prefer = 3–4 points Samplers of the brand = 1–2 points Otherwise = 0 points
Consumers understanding and embracing the brand	. . . . . ./10	Based on brand measurement with consumers, high value = 8–10 points Medium value = 6–7 Below average = 4–5 Low value = 1–3 Otherwise = 0
Consumers asking for additional products or services	. . . . . ./10	If yes = 10 points; if no = 0
Organization achieves superior results	. . . . . ./10	If the company hit financial targets last 12 quarters = 9–10 points 8 quarters = 7–8 points 4 quarters = 4–5 points 2 quarters = 1–2 points Otherwise = 0 points
Total Score	. . . . . ./60	Maximum score = 60 points Above 40, the brand can be considered license-able.

Case # 8 – Laurel Burch Licensing Enters Its Second Decade

Laurel Burch was an American artist born in 1945 in southern California. She began crafting her iconic one-of-a-kind necklaces in San Francisco's Haight-Ashbury in the 1960s. Her art was inspired by her desire to give and her passion to create beauty. It transcended cultures and boundaries of age and race. Her daughter, Aarin, launched Laurel Burch Studios in 2012 five years after Laurel died to continue to share her mother's spirit through products based on her art. The focus here is on an enduring relationship that has delivered substantial value creation in multiple ways over the period of the partnership.

Licensor: Laurel Burch Inspirations, LLC DBA Laurel Burch Studios has the exclusive right to license the Laurel Burch Artwork and Trademarks throughout North America
Licensee: SUN N SAND® ACCESSORIES and other Laurel Burch licensees
Licensed Property: Laurel Burch Artwork and Trademarks
Geographic Area: The US, Canada, Mexico, US Virgin Islands, Guam and Puerto Rico.
Date: April 2022

Situation: Aarin Burch has been leading Laurel Burch Studios for the past ten years. She has witnessed success but has not reached the level she believes is attainable. Her desire is to bring Laurel's messages of connectedness, love, inclusiveness and the celebration of the kindred spirit through her art and the products the art is on to the world, for people from 10 to 80.

Task: To figure out how to reach more people, ultimately "to touch every human!" Aarin wants to come at it from every direction, to make it accessible to the people who know the brand and also to those who are not familiar with the brand. One way is to create new art that appeals to a broader audience.

Action: Aarin is focusing on many categories and making improvements. For the bag line, she has included more contemporary shapes. She has also added new materials, like washed canvas and leather, to expand the category. She plans to bring back sweatshirts and cover-ups from the now-popular 1990s. The hydration category is also important and supports her sustainability mission. Aarin has insisted some items be made in the US.

Results: The brand's longevity comes from staying true to the brand but freshening up with new designs, new art, continued engagement and communication. It also comes from Aarin's enthusiastic approach with her licensees that she gets from her mom. "Everyone gets excited. It's contagious. The licensees say, 'I didn't know we would get this far after your mom passed.'" They now believe in Aarin and the program.

Noteworthy: A key to the success of the Laurel Burch licensing program is the licensees. They focus on product development, conduct research and testing, invest in marketing, hire experts and create licensing plans. They keep Aarin informed on when they are launching a product line, what shows they are at and their intent to add more products. They also keep her abreast of their marketing, advertising plan and use of social media. First and foremost, it is the relationship. "They have a win and I have a win. The best players get that if the brand is healthy they are going to benefit greatly."

References

Adıgüzel, S. (2020). Market and brand positioning and sustainability strategies in international marketing. *International Journal of Scientific Research and Management*, 8(9), 9–24.

Chadwick, S., & Holt, M. (2008). Releasing latent brand equity: The case of UEFA's champions league. *The Marketing Review*, 8(2), 147–162.

Codella, D. (2021). *The winning Coca-Cola formula for a successful campaign*. Wrike.

Conejo, F., & Wooliscroft, B. (2015). Brands defined as semiotic marketing systems. *Journal of Macromarketing*, 35(3), 287–301.

Deeny, G. (2021). Repositioning Ferrari: From license business to lifestyle brand. *Fashion Network*. www.fashionnetwork.com/news/Repositioning-ferrari-from-license-business-to-lifestyle-brand,1310497.html#christian-dior

Halloran, T. (2014). The eight phases of brand love. *Harvard Business Review*. https://hbr.org/2014/02/the-eight-phases-of-brand-love

Hsu, L., Fournier, S., & Srinivasan, S. (2016). Brand architecture strategy and firm value: How leveraging, separating, and distancing the corporate brand affects risk and returns. *Journal of the Academy of Marketing Science*, 44, 261–280.

Keller, K. L., & Brexendorf, T. O. (2019). Strategic brand management process. *Handbuch Markenführung*, 155–175.

Keller, K., & Swaminathan, V. (2019). *Strategic brand management: Building, measuring, and managing brand equity.* Pearson Education.

Kotler, P. T., & Armstrong, G. (2017). *Principles of marketing, eBook, global edition: Principles of marketing.* Pearson Higher Education.

Licensing International Staff. (2023). *Women's world cup teams make a play for licensing.* Licensing International.

Lotman, J. (2020). *Invisible marketing: A hidden tool for connecting with consumers through licensing.* Lioncrest Publishing.

Mackelden, A. (2018, May 28). Kate Middleton just wore a gorgeous and affordable dress on a day out with Prince George. It's from Zara, and it has almost sold out. *Bazaar.* www.harpersbazaar.com/celebrity/latest/a20943813/kate-middleton-dress-day-out-with-prince-george-princess-charlotte/

Martinez, A. (2022). Building a brand strategy: Essentials for long-term success. *MarTech.* https://martech.org/building-a-brand-strategy-essentials-for-long-term-success/

Maurya, U. K., & Mishra, P. (2012). What is a brand? A perspective on brand meaning. *European Journal of Business and Management, 4*(3), 122–133.

Pozzo, B., & Jacometti, V. (2016). *Fashion law-the legal issues of the fashion supply chain.* Giuffrè.

Reid, M., Luxton, S., & Mavondo, F. (2005). The relationship between integrated marketing communication, market orientation, and brand orientation. *Journal of Advertising,* 11–23.

Royce, A. (2023). Kate Middleton's coronation weekend shoes earn $726,000 in media exposure for Aquazzura. *Fashion Network.* https://footwearnews.com/shoes/womens-footwear/kate-middleton-aquazzura-shoes-coronation-1203462162/

Vanamee, N. (2021). *Ferrari shifts into high fashion.* Town & Country.

Wardak, B. (2020, May 15). Michael Jordan: The branding G.O.A.T. *License Global.* www.license-global.com/trends-insights/michael-jordan-branding-goat

Wong, H. I., & Merrilees, B. (2008). The performance benefits of being brand-orientated. *Journal of Product & Brand Management, 17*(6), 372–383.

4

RUNNING A BRAND LICENSING PROGRAM

Learning Objectives

The aim of this chapter is to provide content and tools to answer the following questions: How to implement an effective licensing program? How to choose the licensor and licensee? Which tools can be used to execute the program? After reading this chapter, the readers will be able to: select the partners with whom to enter a licensing program, identify the appropriate tools and apply them for implementing a long-term program, and assess licensor and licensee according to specific metrics.

Keywords: Licensor Assessment Check, Licensee Assessment Check, LASSO Method, Licensing Program Destination Metrics, Application & Projections, Due Diligence, Deal Terms Alignment, Contract Negotiation, Licensing Contract and Deal Memo, Orientation Session, Business Plan & Monitoring, Core Program Elements.

1. How to Choose the Licensor: The LASSO Method

A valuable brand, tailor-made licensing program and a best-in-class licensee can increase the likelihood of a successful long-term deal (Stone, 2018). However, that is not enough without licensing program management, which includes a plan of activities, a set of goals and objectives, metrics and results, monitoring and control systems. Being considered a valuable brand owner or even one that is best-in-class involves more than just having a strong brand with high unaided brand awareness or brand preference. It means developing a solid working relationship between licensor and licensee, learning practices, and processes.

Before choosing the licensor with whom to enter a licensing program, licensees consider several critical aspects for the program success, starting with the activities that belong to the licensor. Tasks of the brand owner are to: manage the licensing program, provide tools and templates for the license to be successful, have an approval process, work closely with their licensees, have best practices, possess references from their current and former

DOI: 10.4324/9781003364566-5

licensees, have strong leadership, deliver on their end of the deal and have a valuable brand that possesses the highest levels of brand loyalty.

There are several additional things for licensees to consider before choosing the licensor with whom to enter into a licensing program, which include:

- Assess the strong brands as they are candidates to be licensed. So, if the brand is not strong, well-known or loved by consumers, it might be better to stop and look for alternative brands to license. If, however, the brand is strong, it will be permitted to extend and expand into categories that complement its original offering.
- Understand that investment risks for the brand owner will be lower with the involvement of licensees that are skilled in manufacturing the product and marketing it in their network of distributors and resellers. In addition to a cost-effective program, licensors will consider whether a licensee allows them to move into new, hard-to-reach categories that could provide additional financial gain.
- Acknowledge that understanding the consumers' wants and devising a solution to satisfy them play a significant role in the brand owners' decision to add a manufacturer to their list of potential licensees. The licensee's prospective products and their distribution channels will be observed and evaluated by the licensor.
- Take into consideration that licensors evaluate potential licensees' ability to enhance the licensed brand and assess the interest level of the prospective licensees and their commitment to making the licensed products. Licensors consider how licensees familiarize themselves with the licensor's brand positioning, promise and architecture. They also consider how many products developed during the evaluation phase include the proposed look and the feel of the licensed products and incorporate the brand's attributes into the design of the products.
- Ensure the deal terms are set in a way that allows both the licensor and the licensee to achieve a successful long-term licensing program. If one party feels that the other is benefiting more from the partnership, chances are that the deal will not succeed in the long term.
- Identify several options of brands from which prospective licensees could acquire a license and set limits on what deal terms they will accept, regardless of the brand.
- Familiarize with the licensor and the licensing program. This includes understanding the approval process, the licensing style guide, reporting requirements, marketing investment expectations and other contractual obligations.

Choosing a licensor who is easy to work with and whose thinking aligns with the licensee reflects on the license. Licensees have the opportunity to decide which brands they desire to build a brand licensing program around. The process of searching and evaluating potential brand owners is approached with the mindset of being a partner who is aware of the advantages and limits that licensing can bring to the company. However, the selection is not straightforward and requires a careful assessment of the brand's potential to expand and the profiles of the brand owners. Once a sufficient number of potential candidates in which to license have been found, they can be evaluated further to determine how successful they will be in a partnership until the final choice is made. Adopting a model based on brand owner attributes can help manufacturers discover brand owners that fall within their standards of a potential candidate.

The selection process includes important steps:

- Identifying and cataloging potential brand owners.
- Developing a checklist of brand parameters.
- Evaluating potential brand owners against the parameters.
- Selecting the brand owner with the product category best suited to the licensee's growth objectives.

The first source to start the brand's research is the brand owner's website. This source provides an ample amount of information about their mission, vision, purpose, financial status and success. It often will also convey the company's managerial and operational philosophy. While public companies are required to file certain financial statements and list them on their websites, these filings are not required for private companies. Therefore, public relations releases, analyst estimates and companies like D&B Hoovers help financially evaluate private companies. Another source includes online business directories such as Manta, LinkedIn Company Directory and Google My Business which can provide extra information about an organization. Portals like Yahoo Finance provide extensive background information about private and public companies and supplementary information, like a new product, how much they spend on market research, the opening of new offices or the entry into new distribution channels. Other sources, specific to the licensing industry, include LIMA, License Global, or Total Licensing. They offer insights into many aspects of a company, which makes it easier to find potential brand owner candidates. Trade Publications, such as *Forbes*, *Entrepreneur* and *BPA* (The Worldwide Brand Report), are another type of platform used for finding potential brand owner prospects. They are written by professionals and reporters that know their industry inside and out. These publications give information on the best-in-class brand owners, including their leadership characteristics, reputation and desired outcomes. They reveal which kind of innovation is upcoming and if they are currently working with other licensees. In addition, there are also several companies that produce published directories. Kazachok, a company based in Paris, has a number of firms in their directory for France and greater Europe. Other useful directories include Toy Directory, Baby and Children's, HFN and Licensing Intelligence. Store Walks are also beneficial resources in this process to see products sold and uncover which brands have a dominant presence in the channels of interest. With the increase of marketplace and digital platforms, virtual store walks are becoming relevant sources of information. Many users and consumers shop comfortably from their homes. Through walks in the virtual shops, it is possible to understand which brands also have a presence in online mass retailer channels, such as AliExpress (Italy), Alibaba (China), Allegro (Poland), Amazon (worldwide), Blocket (Sweden), Bol (Holland), (South Korea), CoupangeBay, Ebay (Australia, Italy), Emag.ro (Poland), Etsy (India), FlipkaKaola (China), Hepsiburada (Middle East), Kmart (Australia), Manomano (Italy), MercadoLibre (Latin America), Olx (Poland), Rakuten (Japan), Shein, Taobao (China), TMall (China), Wildberries (Russia), Zalando (Italy). Trade Shows are another option for finding prospective brand owners, who attend multiple trade shows throughout the year. Oftentimes brand owners are not thinking about licensing their brand; they are more concerned with how to sell their products to their target market, but this makes them fertile ground. Using a combination of all four selection techniques should give a robust list of prospective companies, and the brands they own, in which to pursue a partnership (Goldscheider & Gordon, 2006).

After identifying and cataloging several prospective brand owners, the next step is to develop a basic checklist of parameters that measure each brand. Evaluating the brands against specific components, such as whether they offer sales support or how much they spend on brand marketing, provides clear insights into how these brands operate, and, specifically, whether they are underoptimized, optimized or overoptimized. To this end, the LASSO Method can be used. The LASSO Method is an acronym for Lateral, Addictive, Storied, Scalable, Ownable (Canalichio, 2018).

Lateral: Consider how "lateral" each brand is with respect to categories, product lines and geographical markets. The evaluation of the "Lateral" component is based on the answer to the following questions: What categories can they expand into? Do these categories include licensee products? Have the brand owners expanded their brand(s) into new territories while staying true to the idea for which the brands are renowned? Is the brand too lateral? How strong is the brand? Is there a clear line of sight between what the brand says and stands for, and the products that comprise the brand, everywhere it is seen?

Addictive: Addictiveness gives consumers a way to connect to the brand outside of purchasing the product. Addictiveness generates a unique relationship between the brand and the consumer that promotes healthy growth and revenue. The evaluation of the "addictive" component is based on the following questions: Does the brand have the right combination of frequency, intensity and access? Does the brand keep consumers wanting more? Is it consistently surprising and surprisingly consistent?

Storied: Each brand has a story. What is the story of the selected brands? How does the licensee's product align with, and fit into, each brand's story? Does the brand's story enable fans to feel like they are connected to something that is meaningful and enduring? Does this brand take customers on a journey that feels both familiar and new?

Scalable: Considers the scalability of a brand. Does the brand have the capacity to scale into new territories, markets and sectors? If so, does the licensee's category fit with these territories, markets and sectors? Is the brand owner expanding the brand purposely into territories and sectors that fit with the brand? Is that category growing at a rate that will add critical momentum to the brand? Is there a presence of brand equity, footprint, presence and growth?

Ownable: Own ability decides the form, and the form decides where the brand can go, how easily it can meet the demands of the consumer, and where it can be found. Does this company have their own IP through copyright, patents, trademarks and trade secrets to ensure long-term profitability and maintain market relevance? Do consumers feel like they have "ownership" of this brand? How does the brand owner include licensees, retailers and other partners into decisions that affect the long-term success of the brand?

Measuring the brand against The LASSO Method allows the licensee to recognize if the brand owner is overexpanding into categories that are diluting the equity of the brand. In this case, the chances of the license being a great success are low.

Additional parameters can be added to evaluate brands against components even more accurately. They include:

Organizational Leadership: When evaluating brand owners in this area, the focus is on whether they have had steady leadership over the years or if their leadership has changed substantially during the same period.

Approval Processes: The approval process is a big factor for the licensee. It's important that the approval process is easy to complete and quickly approved.

Financial Health: The overall financial health shows how healthy and robust the brand owners are in their business. Information on financial health is available on specialized databases such as Hoovers and Data Monitor.

Price: Check if the brand owner's prices are aligned with those of the licensee or if they are lower or higher and if they are low-tier, mid-tier or high-tier. If they are aligned, brand owners are in good shape. Otherwise, the lack of price alignment could be problematic in the long term.

After completing the additional parameters, the assessment check for identifying the prospective licensor is complete. The check will enable the licensee to hone down the list of candidates that are going to be best suited for their product.

After having selected potential brand owners, acquired an adequate amount of knowledge about the brand and used the LASSO Method along with additional parameters to evaluate the brand owner, the last step is the interview. It consists of a series of questions to assess abilities, interest level and adaptation between the licensor and the licensee. One approach is to develop a 30–60–90 plan. This is a report that lays out the steps to take in the first 30 days, 60 days and 90 days if a licensing program is run with this brand. A 30–60–90 plan allows the parties to evaluate the feasibility, profitability and brand equity growth. When these steps are finished, the final piece is to conduct a Licensor Assessment Check, as shown in Table 4.1.

TABLE 4.1 Licensor Assessment Check

Licensors Parameters	Expectations
Brand Awareness (Unaided)	High
Brand Marketing Support	Ongoing
Brand Preference (Consumer/End-User)	Strong
Company Reputation	High
Financial Health	Strong and Stable
Licensing Program Management	Straightforward and Efficient
Managerial and Operational Philosophy	Spirit of Partnership
Market Research	Dedicated and Allocated
Outcomes	Win-Win
Sales Support	Committed and Willing

MICKEY MOUSE STAYS EVERGREEN

Mickey Mouse was created in 1928 by Walt Disney and Ub Iwerks. In 1934, at the height of the Depression, General Foods, the makers of Post Toasties, paid $1 million for the right to put Mickey Mouse cut-outs on the back of cereal boxes. In one day, Macy's New York sold a record 11,000 timepieces featuring the Mickey Mouse image. In 2003, Mickey turned 75 years old. America's favorite mouse had lost his connection with consumers and needed to be revitalized. Disney wanted to explore how it could revitalize Mickey with consumers. They used Mickey's birthday to increase Mickey's relevance through a new apparel line. Disney collaborated with the hottest designers to create a high-end vintage program through upscale Los Angeles-based clothing retailer, Fred Segal (Ahrens, 2003). To promote the line, Mickey was seated with celebrities who wore the clothes at marquee events and was featured in top shows including Sex and the City. The program created tremendous buzz and the Mouse was back reviving the character. It also changed the perceptions of Disney as a company, so that it is now viewed as a major fashion player. The program consistently ranks on Women's Wear Daily's WWD100 list of most influential fashion brands. Even more compelling was that the apparel program had no specific entertainment aspect. The program was created simply to remind consumers why they love Mickey Mouse.

2. How to Choose the Licensee: The Assessment Check

The choice of licensees is of strategic importance for the success of an effective and long-lasting licensing program (Canalichio, 2019). Licensors look for licensees that: help in accomplishing their brand licensing goal; believe in the vision of the brand and reap the benefit of establishing the brand in their category; are willing to invest in innovation, product development and marketing; have demonstrated success in the marketplace and achieved category leader status; are well managed and deliver consistent economic and financial results; and possess excellent references from licensors and retailers.

The brand owner selects the licensee based on an evaluation that considers the overall value that the manufacturer can bring to the partnership. Two components are relevant in determining overall value. A first component examines and measures the side of the business that involves the operational aspect of the partnership. Key issues are, for example, leadership, being a category captain, showing financial consistency in the marketplace, growing over time, insights considered relevant for product development and the size of the marketing and distribution investments. The second component is about understanding how the licensee fits with the licensor organization. Critical aspects are, for example, business affinities, shared visions and common values, the way of facing challenges and seizing opportunities. When the two components match with those of the licensor, the probability that the licensee will be selected among the various potential candidates is higher.

The selection process consists of several steps that include: research to identify and catalog potential licensees, development of a checklist of parameters for evaluation; evaluation of potential licensees against the parameters and selection of the most suitable and qualified licensee. Research can be conducted independently or through a third party. Regardless of the route selected, research is critical in understanding who licensees are and their qualities. Sources to start the manufacturers' research are websites, publications, store walks and trade shows. After spotting and cataloging several prospective licensees, licensors develop a basic checklist of parameters for evaluation. Parameters include:

Geographic Reach: Licensors consider whether the licensee is selling in the region the licensor is in or wants to be in. If not, the licensee is not a suitable candidate for the licensor. Having a licensee that is already established in the region that mirrors where the brand is strong and wants to be sold solves many unforeseen issues related to the distribution.

Service: Licensors rate the service level and how well the licensee is servicing customers. For instance, empty shelves give the impression the potential licensee is not servicing customers as it should.

Financial Health: The overall financial health shows how healthy and robust the licensees are in their business. Information on financial health is available on specialized databases such as Hoovers and Data Monitor.

Continuous Improvement: History of innovation provides an overview of where licensees started and where they are going. If they have a track record of making refinements, filing patents and improving products' features and benefits, then that is a good indicator of the propensity to innovate.

Product Scope: Depending on the category selected, having a broad or narrow scope may be suitable for the licensor.

Capacity: What is the manufacturing capacity? Are licensees going to be able to handle the consumers' demand for the brand in the present channels? If the brand is enjoyed by many, one can assume that demand for the product will increase substantially. To meet this demand, substantial investment and more extensive distribution systems are required.

History: Licensors want to understand where the organization started, where it is now, and how it got there. What is the company's history? Is the company licensed with other brands? If so, who? Licensors tend to focus on whether licensees have had a history of market success.

Channel Reach: Are licensees selling in the channels that the licensor desires? Do they have a category captain status in that specific channel? If so, then the licensors know they are going to have a better chance of success.

Price: Does licensees' pricing align with the licensor's pricing? Is it low-tier, mid-tier or high-tier? How do prices compare with the licensor's price? Are they aligned? If so, licensees are in good shape. Table 4.2, the Licensee Assessment Check, reports the level of expectations for the parameters used in the assessment check that licensees will be up against.

The assessment check enables the licensor to hone down the list of candidates that are going to be best suited for their brand. Once the checklist is established, the next step is for the licensor to conduct an interview with the selected licensees to assess their level of interest. To summarize, brand owners will identify best-suited licensees to extend their brand. As the licensor searches for potential candidates, they will research the prospective candidates through their website, trade publications, store walks and trade shows. Licensees should be sure to have positioned themselves in these areas and have provided a clear overview of their capabilities. Once the licensor has previewed potential licensees, they will evaluate them against certain parameters they have developed based on several factors. These parameters will help to determine the qualified partner.

TABLE 4.2 Licensee Assessment Check

Licensees Parameters	Expectations
Geographic Reach	Extensive Service High
Financial Health	Strong
Innovation	Strong
Continuous Improvement	Ongoing
Quality	High
Product Scope	Broad
Capacity	Available
History Market	Success
Channel Reach	Broad
Price	Aligned with Channel

BOB THE BUILDER *GETS COURTED BY HASBRO*

In the late 1990s there was no children's television entertainment property like *Bob the Builder* in the US market. There were preschool brands like Teletubbies, but the style of animation for *Bob the Builder* was different. The characters actually looked like toys. In 1999 HIT Entertainment, a UK-based company that owned the property, finalized the broadcast rights with Nickelodeon for the US market. As soon as the news broke, senior executives at Hasbro and Mattel expressed their interest in acquiring the toy license. Both were great companies but only the right choice would propel the *Bob the Builder* property and ensure its long-term success. Hasbro's vision was to create a "preschool world" across multiple toy categories which could enable HIT Entertainment to get a footing in the US preschool market. Mattel was interested in the anthropomorphic style of the vehicles as a way to support their *Hot Wheels* and *Matchbox* brands. Financially the offers were comparable, but the strategic vision of Hasbro to create a larger footprint for the *Bob the Builder* brand across multiple preschool products and categories influenced the decision. Hasbro's CEO, Alan Hassenfeld, reached out to Holly Stein Shulman, Global Merchandise Licensing Vice President, HIT Entertainment, to assure her how dedicated Hasbro was to making the licensing program a success. Hassenfeld advised her that Hasbro would treat *Bob the Builder* like their own brand, that they were in it for the long haul and that they were committed to being the best toy partner. While this had a positive influence, the gesture that solidified Stein Shulman's decision occurred when Hasbro invited her and other HIT Entertainment colleagues to tour Hasbro's offices in 2000 at the International Toy Fair held in New York City. During the visit, the group was invited to meet with Hassenfeld. According to Stein Shulman, "When we walked into Alan's office, he was fully dressed as *Bob the Builder* – overalls, tool belt, hard hat and all!" That sealed the deal. Hasbro's toy program would go on to be hugely successful, catapulting the *Bob the Builder* franchise across multiple licensed categories and products for years to come (Canalichio, 2018).

3. Strategic Components of Brand Licensing Programs

Key issues in brand licensing programs are understanding what the destination for the licensing program looks like and implementing tools and templates that will enable the licensor to reach that destination (Santo, 2015). While not exhaustive, the following questions help dimensionalize strategic issues to consider in executing a brand licensing program:

- How does a brand licensing program support the brands being licensed? There are several factors to take into consideration: the non-monetary benefits of a program, including building brand equity, gaining brand presence in retail and through licensee marketing activities, entering new categories, penetrating into new channels and opening new geographical markets; the monetary benefits of capturing royalty revenue, reporting sales of licensed merchandise and benefiting from contractually required marketing budgets from licensees; and the legal benefits of maintaining and protecting trademark rights in a particular category through active commerce.
- How does a licensor define success – over 1 year, 3 years, 5 years? Some key metrics to define and set benchmarks against include: brand equity, brand protection, number of categories, level of innovation, licensed merchandise sales targets, channels of distribution, range of royalty rates and the amount of royalties. For each benchmark, the licensor will set the appropriate metric and then measure that benchmark at the time horizon to determine if the program fails to meet, meets or exceeds that metric. There can be some situations where the program meets or exceeds one or more standards but fails to meet others. In these instances, the licensor may choose to modify their strategies to correct for the shortfall.
- How does licensing fit into the licensor's organization? What department is responsible for the activity? Licensing normally is managed by the marketing department, business development or the legal department depending on the objective of the program. If the program is designed to strengthen the brand, it normally falls under the marketing department. If it is designed to maximize royalty revenue, it gets managed by the business development group. If protection of the trademark is the priority, then the legal department usually oversees it. If the licensor has the capability or desires to build the competency in house, the licensing activity could be conducted internally. Otherwise, if the goal is to build a presence in a series of categories more quickly, the licensor may choose to outsource the function. When managed in-house, it is important to determine who will oversee the day-to-day management of the licensing program. Each specific task takes a specific skill set, so the person responsible for prospecting and the vetting likely will not have the appropriate skills to conduct and track the approvals. Similarly the responsible for negotiating the deal terms may or may not be the one responsible for writing the contracts. Finally, tracking the sales of the licensed merchandise and the royalties requires different skills than is required to ensure the royalties are collected.
- Where should digital and physical, that is, prototype submissions be stored? There are normally three stages of approvals – concept, prototype and final production – which require a submission by the licensee. For the concept stage, a two-dimensional image is submitted. For the prototype and final production stages, a three-dimensional product is submitted. These submissions are stored in a location to allow for access if there is a question as to the quality of a product (Raugust, 2004). For many businesses and industries, keeping licensing submissions for a minimum of three to five years

is recommended. This time frame allows for compliance with potential audits, legal inquiries or regulatory requirements.

- How is testing conducted and who establishes the standards? If the licensed product falls within a category where the licensor has competency, then often the licensor will set the standard and test the prototype and final production run samples in-house to ensure they meet the minimum standards. If the licensed product falls outside of the competency of the licensor, then a recognized testing organization will be used to establish the testing standards and conduct the tests to ensure the product is compliant. In each instance the testing authority will advise the licensee whether the sample met the standard or if it has to modify the product to be compliant. For many businesses and industries, keeping test results for a minimum of three to five years is recommended. This time frame allows for compliance with potential audits, legal inquiries or regulatory requirements.

- What are brand licensing software management systems? Brand licensing software management systems aim to simplify the complex process of managing brand licensing relationships, protect the integrity of the brand and maximize the value of brand assets through effective licensing strategies. These systems can be valuable for companies with extensive brand portfolios or those involved in licensing their brands across different industries and regions. Often licensing software platforms have a variety of modules designed to optimize contract management, asset management, royalty calculation, approval workflows, reporting, compliance monitoring and IP management.

The first step of the destination program definition is to set the parameters that characterize the content of the licensing program (Table 4.3). The Licensing Program Destination

TABLE 4.3 Licensing Program Destination Metrics

Program Parameters	Expectations
Core Objective	Brand Protection | Brand Equity | Royalty Revenue
Oversight	Legal | Marketing | Business Development
Staffing	In House | Outsource (Agency)
Category Selection	Reinforces Brand Expansion Point℠ and Promise
Brand Equity Metrics	Maintain or Grow
Brand Protection	Minimum Standard
Category Growth	By Channel | Geographic | Stock Keeping Unit
Innovation	In Line with Brand Standards
Licensee Channel Penetration	In 2 of Top 5 Retailers for Each Channel Authorized
Stock Keeping Unit Penetration	Top 2 SKUs < 50% of Retail Sales Per Licensee
Royalty Rates	In Line with Brand Standards | 25% of Expected Profits
Retailer Relations	In Line with Standards Set by Retailer, Licensor and Licensee
Royalties Earned	In Line with Licensee Business Plan
Sales (Licensed Merchandise)	In Line with Licensee Business Plan
Approval Phases	Concept | Prototype | Final Production
Product Testing	Internal Standard | Recognized International Authority

Metrics table identifies those parameters that are of strategic importance. The parameters range from purpose to operations to standards to benchmarks to implementation. Having a clear understanding of each guides a licensor on how to run the brand licensing program to achieve their objectives. There is no right way to operate a brand licensing program; rather, it depends on what the objectives are to achieve success. However, there are some parameters that are important to maintain such as category selection, brand protection and innovation regardless of the objectives. Table 4.3 shows program parameters and the relative expectations. For royalty rates, the 25 percent rule is considered a good benchmark for setting royalty rates in the absence of established industry standards or brand licensing program (Parr, 2007, pp. 21–22).

Once the above parameters are set, the licensor conducts a current reality assessment to evaluate the status of the licensing program and determines if, and where, there is a gap. Developing a strategic plan is one way to close the gap between the destination program parameters and expectations. In the strategic plan priorities, milestones and timelines are set so success can be measured over a designated time horizon.

One ongoing strategic parameter that is critical to the success of the licensing program is the relationship between the licensor and the licensee. A way to ensure both parties are satisfied is to establish routine and frequent touch points. This includes an annual business review, and then quarterly, monthly and biweekly meetings. These ensure both parties' needs, and commitments are met at a strategic and tactical level. This cadence also helps ensure the terms of the licensing agreement are met. If there are any product recalls or lawsuits that arise, an emergency meeting can be scheduled to address the issue with minimum disruption to the program.

LESSONS LEARNED BY AARIN BURCH – CEO LAUREL BURCH STUDIOS WHILE RUNNING HER LICENSING PROGRAMS

In this interview of April 22, 2022, Pete Canalichio, brand strategist and licensing expert, discusses with Aarin Burch, CEO Laurel Burch Studios, about the brand's longevity and the importance of it staying true while remaining fresh and relevant. The interview, which took place over Zoom connecting Pete in his office in Atlanta and Aarin in Berkeley, lasted approximately one hour. In this interview Aarin speaks about the process of building an enduring licensing program. She speaks about her brand, highlighting two components: the relevance of the brand and the art of figuring out how to connect that brand to a consumer in a consistently surprising and surprisingly consistent way. She mentions the importance of the role of retailers in supporting the brand's goals of staying relevant and connected. The first part is about having a group of outstanding retailers that know their shoppers and end users, are committed to the Laurel Burch brand, and are willing to collaborate with Aarin and position Laurel Burch in their stores for success. In addition, Aarin mentions the role of her licensees. She reflects on the importance of having a strong group of licensees who know their customers and consumers; Aarin emphasizes the importance of supporting them, working in a spirit of collaboration and true partnership, setting them up for success, building integrity and trust with them.

TABLE 4.4 The Importance of Strategic Components for Ensuring Licensing Longevity

Topic	Aarin Burch's answers
Laurel Burch brand promise	It's to bring Laurel's messages and art to the world. "We share these messages to express our interconnectedness. Our products are created in hopes of ensuring that people feel loved seen and celebrated." By owning something she created, one feels a part of something bigger and through this connection will want to share the Laurel Burch art with someone else so they can feel the same.
Laurel Burch target audience	The messages and art of Laurel Burch are created for everyone, from the 10-year-old to the 80-year-old. Laurel Burch's art inspires connectedness, love, inclusiveness and a celebration of the kindred spirit. The people drawn to it are the 50- to 80-year-olds who knew Laurel Burch's work, but her art transcends generations. Their grandchildren think it is cool and retro. The licensed products touch people in a powerful way and have been known to bring them to tears.
Goal of the Laurel Burch brand strategy	It's to figure out how to reach more people and impact their lives. "I am trying to come at it from every direction," Aarin shares. "We want to make the brand accessible to as many people as possible." One way Aarin is doing this is by reimagining the art. With the changes in technology driving higher resolution, there is more clarity and vibrancy. Digital printing enables her to add more detail and colors. "I can create a brand-new cat design or bring back that exact cat my mother created." If people are not familiar with the brand right away they are thrilled when they learn of the brand's 50-year history. "This is the real deal, just like Sassoon and Klein."
How the Laurel Burch brand grew	"When I first took over the brand, I wanted to take it to a new and younger audience, so I added iPhone cases, skins for computers, water bottles and backpacks. I added contemporary shapes to my bag line. I also considered new materials like washed canvas and leather to expand the category," explains Aarin. The challenge for her was how to reach a younger audience while maintaining customers who were now in their late 70s. With so much appeal and such a rich history, Aarin focused on what was most important: the story, the connectedness, the vibrancy and the relevance. The combination has allowed her to grow the Laurel Burch brand in new and meaningful ways.

(Continued)

TABLE 4.4 (Continued)

Topic	Aarin Burch's answers
Laurel Burch's source of inspiration	Laurel Burch source of inspiration began with her purpose: to create art that connects with people, that helps them feel loved and seen. Her art and message were, and remain, universal. For this reason, retailers around the globe were interested. "In addition to North America, my mom sold to stores in Japan, Australia, and Europe," explains Aarin. Laurel not only created products, but she created events that brought her vision to life. She produced incredible events in Macy's, Emporium and Bloomingdales. Another concept she created was opening themed restaurants locally that offered guests an immersive experience in another country, some as exotic as Morocco. "She wanted everything to be a full experience, from the dancers to the art, to the dishes, and to the staff engagement." In addition to these concepts, Laurel Burch cared about communities. They provided an inspiration for her work. She supported numerous organizations and causes like the SPCA, BOK Ranch, HIV, September 11 and Conservation International. She cared about people and the planet and got involved in events supporting Earth Day and breast cancer awareness. Laurel also had a passion for the performing arts. Her interests were expansive – many of them centered on women, their relevance and importance. She brought women together across the world, by recognizing their value and contribution.
What the Laurel Burch licensing program entails	"What it comes down to is taking Laurel Burch art and putting it on a variety of products in a meaningful and purposeful way. That's the most basic part of it. This includes not only creating products but telling a story and reaching the right audience with those products."
The most important contributors to the Laurel Burch brand licensing program	"You are not just buying something off the shelf. The intention is for you to realize this comes from an artist and created purposefully to support you in feeling good, and positive in the world." "My licensees were drawn to the brand because of my mother, the beauty of the art and her intention with it. To keep it on the right course, I have to be intentional. The licensees make products and sell them. I have to support them. I am here for them, helping to ensure the products they create are attractive and appealing to their retailers. When they know it's me, her daughter, it gives them confidence. Again and again, they will tell me they are happy with the direction I am taking the company in this new era."

Topic	Aarin Burch's answers
	"Our customers feel that I listen to their opinions. They make suggestions and we pay attention to them. So how do I keep this personal touch and scale at the same time? How do I work smarter and move the needle? I just keep moving forward and trusting my gut. I also hire smart people."
	"Maintaining that personal touch is really important to me. As busy as I am I make every effort to communicate directly with my licensees, retailers and consumers. I don't want buying Laurel Burch to be robotic for consumers. I don't want to be 'untouchable' like Michael Kohrs or Tory Burch. Those retailers often won't call you back. As I scale, I have to figure out a way to keep this connection."
What are the attributes of the best licensees you have known	"My best licensees recognize the beauty of the art my mother created. Together, we say 'Wow!' We are on the same page. They see the beauty and potential. And they have a clear plan for how they will use the art."
What are the attributes of the worst licensees you have known, and why	"They just want to 'put a cat on something.' It's been my greatest apprehension with licensees. It's a hard lesson. I allowed them early on to do what they wanted. Some licensees want to make as much money as possible. Allowing them to 'logo slap' has not been a good decision for me. It would have been better to have started with a smaller program and add to it rather than with 300 Stock Keeping Units. We should have started with 18, then 24 and then scale. This has been one of my biggest lessons."
What things make you excited about your licensees	"The ones I am excited about are the licensees that spend time in product development. They conduct research, testing and take the time to analyze it. They invest in marketing. They hire experts to ensure they are making the best products," offers Aarin. "I get excited when a licensee has a plan, when they tell me when they are launching, what shows they will be at, when they plan to add more product, what their advertising plans are, and how they are using social media. I want to make sure they are using all of the tools. In the past, the licensees would make the product, go to the shows and wait for orders to come. Today, there are so many ways to get out there. First and foremost, it requires they build a relationship with their customers. The best partners get that if the brand is healthy they are going to benefit the most."

(Continued)

TABLE 4.4 (Continued)

Topic	Aarin Burch's answers
What are the attributes of the best-in-class licensee	"We have like minds. They have a genuine love for what we are creating. It isn't just about the numbers. They have to be behind the story and the art. They have a really good distribution plan with identified channels. In the past, I have chosen some who were enthusiastic but didn't have the channels to place the product. Just because they can create a good product doesn't mean they can sell it. Another attribute is that they know their customers, what they want and how to get new customers. Finally, they want to have strong communication with me. This ensures we build something successfully together."
What drives the success of the licensing program	"The success of our licensing program is contingent upon the strength of our licensees. It is driven by their operational excellence, their commitment to our brand and their partnership with our company. It's not enough they are excited and driven; they also have to possess operational excellence. One of my licensees was enthusiastic about our program and asked for the contractual right to go into a new category. They created a great product, but they didn't have the funnel, the distribution or the experience. In the end, it wasn't successful. To ensure a successful licensing program, each licensee must possess all these qualities."
What is the core characteristic or attribute that has contributed more than others to the brand longevity	"The brand's longevity begins with new designs, new art, continued engagement, and communication. When I am enthusiastic and present new art and designs to our licensees, they are going to be enthusiastic. This was true for my mom, too. Everyone gets excited. It's contagious. The most energy and excitement comes from the ones that know what is working. I will bring them something and say, let's try this. They immediately know it is going to work. It is the most fun part. My licensees tell me, 'I didn't know we would get this far after your mom passed.' It's their belief in me that contributes significantly to the brand's longevity."
Critical issues that emerged from the brand licensing programs implemented	"I have some licensees that I don't talk to frequently. In these instances, trusting in the sales and royalty reporting process can be challenging. They have to report their figures accurately. I have to have trust that they will pay me for everything they sell. The best approach is to be in close contact with them. That way, I can build a relationship and establish a level of integrity."

4. Tools to Evaluate Brand Licensing Strategy

Tools and templates for establishing a brand licensing program include: Application & Projections, Due Diligence, Deal Terms Alignment, Contract Negotiation, Licensing Contract and Deal Memo, Orientation Session, Business Plan & Monitoring, Core program elements (Licensing Style Guide & Look Book, Licensing Pitch Deck & Sales Sheet, Licensing Website Tab and Supporting Marketing Materials).

The *licensee application, forecasting guide and vetting tools* are submitted by licensees (Figure 4.1). The *licensee application* is a tool used by licensors to determine licensee motives and to provide them with in-depth information on the licensee's organization in the following areas: Strategic, Financial, Legal and References. The *forecasting guide* provides the licensor with a three-year detailed licensee forecast by region, channel, retailer, SKUs and annual product innovation. The forecast and its viability are compared across licensee candidates to see which, if any, meet the licensor's standards. The licensor uses vetting tools to assess the worthiness of each licensee candidate.

After a prospective licensee completes an application, it's critical that a licensor evaluates the prospective licensee's profile. This requires conducting comprehensive *due diligence* on the selected company from multiple perspectives: business, financial, legal and risk management. The more comprehensive the review, the less likely it is that the licensee will have unforeseen issues going forward, and the greater the likelihood for success. Here are six necessary steps for qualification:

- *Legal Check* – This section aims to answer the following questions in legal and corporate matters: Is the company a legitimate legal entity? How long has it been in business? Where is it incorporated? Is it doing business under a different name? What is its

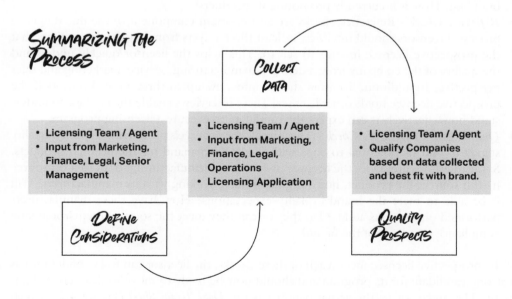

FIGURE 4.1   Licensor Vetting Process

structure? Is it a shell corporation, or does it have actual employees, assets and liabilities? Has it been the subject of any major lawsuits in the last three to five years? If so, what was the nature of the charges and how did the company resolve them?

- *Financial Check* – To fully understand the financial strength of an organization, it's important to obtain the prospective licensee's financial statements going back at least three years. These statements help assure the licensor that the licensee has the resources to commit to the licensing program from the beginning to the end of the contract, and beyond. Many licensed products have a long shelf-life so it is important for the parties to be viable for a minimum of five years after a licensing agreement expires to mitigate any liability.
- *Credit Check* – This reveals the prospective licensee's timeliness and reliability to pay bills. Given the systematic royalty payment requirements of the licensing contract, ascertaining credit-worthiness is critical.
- *Business Check* – This section is about evaluating previous licensing experience to assess the licensee's reliability, skills and ability to collaborate: Is the company reputable in the selected product category? Does it possess any other brand licenses, or has it had them in the past? If so, what do current, or previous licensors say about the way the company has managed its licensing programs? What is its reputation in the marketplace? What do current customers say about its reliability and serviceability? How well managed is the company? How eager is it to get the license? How collaborative? What are the estimated sales forecasts for the selected product, as well as its sales history, over the past three years?
- *Marketing Check* – This reveals the prospective licensee's market position and competitiveness. Some questions are: What is the prospective licensee's market share position in the selected product category? How long has it been selling the product? What is its rank by revenue, distribution, employees? Is it a market leader? What channels is it presently in? How has it been growing? What kind of product innovations has it launched in the past? What are its strengths? How well does it understand the marketplace and branding? How is it currently promoting its products?
- *Reference Check* – Reference checks are an important component of the due diligence process. Licensors should interview at least three buyers from among the retailers that the prospective licensee intends to sell to. This helps the licensor quickly understand the quality of the company from a delivery, manufacturing, service, marketing and sales perspective. In addition, licensors should interview up to three other licensors if the prospective licensee holds other licenses. These interviews enable the licensor to understand how effectively it can expect the candidate to execute a licensing program.
- *Quality and Compliance Check* – This reveals the licensee's production capacity, quality standards and its potential to cope with increased demand for the licensed products. Some questions are: Does the licensee own its own manufacturing, or does it outsource it? If it sources the product, how long has it been working with its manufacturers? Will it be able to meet the brand's quality expectations? How have these manufacturers performed on previous audits? Do they or can they meet the social and environmental compliance standards of the brand?

If the prospective licensee meets each of these checks, the licensor can feel confident it has a strong candidate for its program and should now be ready to move to deal terms alignment. The precursor to the actual contract is the *Deal Terms Sheet* (Figure 4.2), which contains the most important deal terms that the licensee and the licensor need to agree upon. These deal terms, including trademarks licensed, covered products, territories, channels, royalty rates and so on, are terms that both parties will encounter during the day-to-day servicing of the license. A Deal Terms Sheet is reported below. The entire Deal Terms Sheet is reported in Appendix 4.1.

After the licensor and the licensee have understood all the deal terms and have structured a negotiation strategy in their mind, it is time to negotiate each of the deal terms. Only when they agree on each of the deal terms will their relationship reach the next level of actually drafting and signing the contract. The negotiation of the key deal terms involves a meeting between the parties. Communication is an important piece of the negotiation's framework. If both parties have thought through their negotiation's strategy in advance – that is, evaluated their alternatives, defined their Best Alternative to a *Negotiated Agreement*

DEAL TERM SUMMARY SHEET

Date: ___ ___ / ___ ___ / ___ ___ ___ ___

This deal term summary sets forth certain deal terms for a proposed license agreement between the parties. The parties agree that this summary is not a contract and is not binding on either party.

Proposed Licensee:

Licensee address:

Type of entity and state under which Licensee is formed (e.g., a Delaware corporation):

Scope of License

Trademarks:

Covered Products:

Authorized Channels:

FIGURE 4.2   Deal Terms Sheet

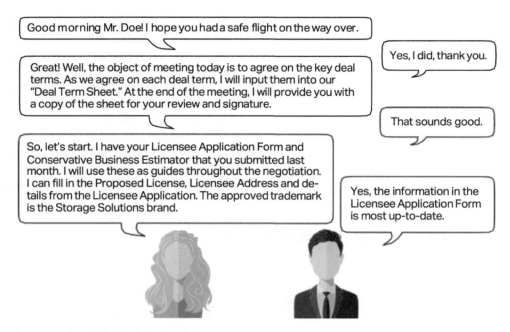

FIGURE 4.3 The Mock Negotiation Sheet

(BATNA) and their interests – an agreement on the Deal Terms Sheet can be achieved in a short time. The mock negotiation below (Figure 4.3) is between Ms. Zerrillo, VP of Licensing for the Storage Solutions Brand (the licensor), and Mr. Doe, the CEO of Excellent Cabinets Corp. (prospective licensee). Excellent Cabinets is interested in licensing the Storage Solutions brand in the Ready-to-Assemble Wooden Shelves and Cabinets category. Excellent Cabinets is a well-respected company and already holds licenses of other prestigious brands in the category, including Shelves!, Woodblocker, Self Shelf, Garage Essentials and Storage Essentials. The entire mock negotiation is reported in Appendix 4.2.

Typically, the licensor's team gets approval from the CEO or the senior management of their company before they can sign the contract (*Licensing Contract*). This stage may be overlooked for smaller-sized deals. In the case of larger deals, where the expected royalty revenue exceeds $1 million, a memo outlining the details of the agreement is prepared by the licensing team and with the help of the business unit that is licensing their brand. The key questions addressed in the memo are: Can the licensee deliver reliable quality and service levels? How will it help the brand? Does the financial return justify time and total efforts?

The *Licensing Deal Memo* (Figure 4.4) contains background information on the product category, such as the size of the market, the players, success factors and consumer insight. It covers the history of the product category and the brand and makes a case for why the chosen product category is a good fit for the brand and the company. It addresses the rationale behind licensing the category as opposed to manufacturing or sourcing it, and why it makes sense to invest in the project. Included with the memo is a summary of the licensing agreement, any pictures of the current product made by the licensee and physical samples, if available. The licensee must keep in mind that even though the licensee has

SAMPLE: MEMO TO THE CEO

To: [Name] CEO

From: [Name] VP of Licensing

Cc: **Head of STORAGE SOLUTIONS Brand**
                Brand Manager of STORAGE SOLUTIONS Brand

Subject: **Licensing Approval Request: Licensee, EXCELLENT CABINETS, for STORAGE SOLUTIONS Branded Ready to Assemble (RTA) wooden garage cabinets and shelves**

Date: March 10, 2024

Sir,

We have a signed contract from Excellent Cabinets, Corp. to license RTA wooden garage cabinets and shelves under the STORAGE SOLUTIONS brand. This license will enable STORAGE SOLUTIONS to improve its current cabinets and shelves product line while maximizing profitability. Immediate execution of this contract is necessary to capture 2025 opportunities.

FIGURE 4.4   Licensing Senior Executive Approval Memo

signed the Deal Terms Sheet, the licensor can walk away from the agreement at any point. Typically, the licensor needs approval from their senior management before they can sign off on any deal. The entire sample of Licensing Senior Executive Approval Memo is reported in Appendix 4.3.

Shortly after the contract has been signed, a formal *orientation session* can be scheduled and conducted. An important reason to conduct an orientation is it helps build an ongoing relationship between the licensor and the licensee. Another reason is that there are a host of requirements laid out in the licensing agreement that are intended to make the program successful. This ranges from understanding the brand, to getting the products approved, to commercializing the product in the marketplace. Doing this effectively requires a great number of personnel from both the licensor and the licensee. The Orientation Process allows for both parties to grasp this understanding. The licensee is responsible for the most crucial asset of the licensor's company, which is their brand. Therefore, the licensee requires a deep understanding of the brand. In addition, the licensee builds the attributes of the brand into the licensed products it intends to create, obtain the requisite approvals in the right way and follow the guidelines. The Orientation Process ensures the commercialization of the licensed product in the category takes place. The orientation creates an opportunity for the licensee to reveal to the licensor the new officially licensed products entering the marketplace that consumers are desiring and demanding. Finally, the Orientation Process helps ensure that the licensee meets the contract obligations.

Thus, the goal of the Orientation Process is to aid in the long-term success of the partnership from its outset. The licensor achieves this by (1) identifying the roles and responsibilities of the parties on the licensor side and ensuring do the same for the licensee side, (2) getting everyone up to speed on their obligations and (3) ensuring the parties on both sides know each other and their respective roles. Up to this point, only one or two people have been involved in establishing the license and have a familiarity about what has happened and what has been required. The orientation (Figure 4.5) enables the employees from both companies responsible for the successful execution of the license to get aligned, up to speed and ready to go. The entire sample of Orientation Meeting Agenda is reported in Appendix 4.4.

The business plan created is a critical component for the brand licensing program success. When the licensor works side-by-side with the licensee and monitors the success of their business with their brand in the marketplace, he/she will learn how to understand the licensee's business plans and ensure alignment with their own business objectives to develop steps toward success.

Once the contract is signed and the licensor makes sure the licensee has a good understanding of the brand, it is essential to give the licensee the right tools to be successful. Monitoring the licensee's business and ensuring that they set achievable targets

Licensor – Licensee Orientation Meeting

Agenda – [Date]

Licensee Attendees:
[Name] – Chief Marketing Officer
[Name] – VP Brand
[Name] – VP Digital
[Name] – VP or Director Product Development
[Name] – VP or Director Partnership
[Name] – Account / Licensing Manager

Licensor Attendees:
[Name] – VP Product Innovation / Research
[Name] – VP Brand / Digital
[Name] – VP Business Development
[Name] – VP Marketing Communications
[Name] – VP or Director Innovation
[Name] – VP or Director of Licensing
[Name] – Director of Operations

Topic	Time	Lead
Welcome Message	9:00am	[Senior Executive, Licensor]
Introductions	9:15am	All Members
Voice of the [Licensor] Brand	9:30am	VP Marketing Communications [Licensor]
Voice of [Licensee] Brand	9:45am	VP Brand [Licensee, if applicable]
Licensee Program Positioning Proposals and discussion	10:00am	Product Branding Examples by Channel VP Product Development [Licensee]

FIGURE 4.5 Orientation Meeting Agenda

empowers the licensee to maximize the license. From a business planning perspective, this entails Sales Management, Marketing Management, and Quality and Compliance Management. Sales Management business planning can be broken down into annual, quarterly or monthly business plans. An Annual Business Plan traditionally gets developed in the third quarter of the prior year to the next year's business plan. While Sales Management business planning can be broken down into quarters, the Marketing Management planning is generally created as an Annual Business Plan. In this Annual Business Plan, the licensee should explain what they intend to do with the brand in that category, what they are going to spend to achieve their goals and how they will align the marketing mix with your own brand marketing. Once discussed, they should then agree to the budget, and how the budget will be spent. Quality and Compliance Management is not broken down quarterly or annually; it's an ongoing planning. This critical piece makes sure that the quality of the products improves or is maintained through an ongoing program that's established by the licensee's quality team on a daily or weekly basis.

The *Annual Business Plan*, for the licensee, is typically developed in the third quarter of the year prior to when the plan is being invoked. Once developed it will be reviewed by the key management team of the licensee and then shared with the licensor. The materials that are included in this plan are traditionally what are included in any business plan. The template provided will share the minimum requirements needed to achieve the revenue goals. The key elements included in the Annual Business Plan are Sales Forecast, Royalty Forecast, Line Review Dates and other Key Retailer Dates. The Sales and Royalty Forecasts are represented by region, channel and product. Line Review Dates focus on the dates that the licensee will meet with the retailer to discuss the products and sales. The Key Retailer Dates include major presentations, initiatives that are being done and innovative products that they should consider as part of their updated modular set in the ongoing sales of your licensed product in their stores. Below is a snapshot of the Annual Business Planning Template (Figure 4.6). The entire Annual Business Planning Template is reported in Appendix 4.5.

The *Brand Licensing Software* for monitoring includes an Application Workflow (the primary purpose is to vet Prospect licensees), Contract Workflow (the primary purpose is to negotiate the licensing agreement), the Approvals Workflow (the primary purpose is to tracks the approval process), the Royalty Management module (primary purpose is to manage royalties due to the licensor from the licensee) and the Brand Protection module (primary purpose is to monitors infringements to the license). Once a licensing software is selected and installed, the licensor and the licensee should undergo training to ensure the parties know how it is to be used.

Finally, it is important to have a *set of core program elements* including a *Licensing Style Guide & Look Book, Licensing Pitch Deck & Sales Sheet, Licensing Website Tab and Supporting Marketing Materials*. The creation of a *brand Style Guide & Look Book* serves two primary purposes. It bridges the gap for prospective licensees to see the complete vision and opportunity of the brand and how it can positively impact sales, and it provides the fundamentals of the brand including how it is physically represented, additionally giving creative direction for how the brand represents and communicates to customers. The *Pitch Deck & Sales Sheet* enables the licensor to grab the attention of any prospective licensee. The Pitch Deck is where the licensor makes the case for how

Annual Business Planning Template

Establishing A Business Plan

The business plan created is a critical component in ensuring the success of your brand licensing program. When you work side-by-side with the licensee and monitor the success of their business with your brand in the marketplace, you will enhance your success. In this memo, you will learn how to understand your licensee´s business plans and ensure alignment with your own business objectives to develop steps towards success.

Once you have signed the contract and made sure the licensee has a good understanding of the brand, it is essential to give the license the right tools to be successful. Monitoring the licensee's business and ensuring that they set achievable targets empowers the licensee to maximize the license. From a business planning perspective, this entails Sales Management, Marketing Management, and Quality and Compliance Management. **Sales Management** business planning can be broken down into annual, quarterly, or monthly business plans. An Annual Business Plan traditionally gets developed in the third-quarter of the prior year to the next year's business plan. While Sales Management business planning can be broken down into quarters, the **Marketing Management** planning is generally created as an annual business plan. In this Annual Business Plan, the licensee should explain what they intend to do with the brand

FIGURE 4.6   Annual Business Planning Template

a licensing partnership will be win-win. The template includes all specific licensee and retailer information. A well-crafted *Sales Sheet* can entice prospective licensees to have a conversation about their business. The *Website Tab* serves as a key sales tool; the web page or tab is an extension of other sales tools. It is integral to capturing inquiries, providing a format for prospects and sharing how licensing would benefit their business. *Supporting Marketing Materials* are additional tools in the licensor's toolbox to drive awareness and communicate the opportunity to prospects. They include a Marketing & Awareness Tool Kit consisting of a social media post graphics & supporting copy, email graphics driving awareness, consideration, and conversion, and trade publication and mock-ups.

Once the licensor has implemented all the tools and templates, he is in a good place to develop several potential categories through existing brand expansion and extension research, insights derived from the data collected, and evaluation of licensor competitors. Once the licensor has completed this, he is in a position to assess categories and derive a set of "qualified" categories by applying the Brand Expansion Point℠ and Architecture filters. The process continues with the production of a qualified list. The Brand Expansion Point is a pivotal characteristic that translates powerfully from one product variant to another, or from one category to another, to give consumers even more of what they want from a brand. The Brand Expansion Point℠ is a powerful emotion or association bonded with that brand that people have" (Canalichio, 2018). Applying the Brand Architecture (Brand Purpose, Brand Personality, Emotional Benefits, Functional

Benefits, Key Product Attribute/Criteria) involves filtering the categories by asking the following questions:

- Do the categories reinforce the brand promise?
- Do the categories pivot around the Brand Expansion Point℠?
- Does the prospective category hurt the parent brand?
- Does the parent brand hurt the prospective category expansion?

From this set of qualified categories, the licensor establishes a scale of priorities for maximizing the impact and develops brand expansion strategy using the following criteria:

- Existing categories where licensor brand is present.
- Categories that are a natural complement to existing categories.
- Biggest opportunities from a brand building and royalty growth perspective.
- Prospective licensee interest.

The final step is for the licensor to implement the licensing program by:

- Incorporating the recommended tools and templates into licensor visual standards.
- Installing the licensing software, training the licensor and licensing agency, as applicable.
- Developing key program elements needed to launch the licensor's brand licensing program.
- Prioritizing the qualified categories based on fit with the licensor brand and potential royalty revenue.
- Identifying a list of prospective licensees that align with licensor standards.
- Prosecuting the list and signing licensees.

Table 4.5 is a chart that articulates the activity and estimated time frame to implement these practices.

TABLE 4.5 Brand Licensing Implementation Schedule

Activity	Month 1	Month 2	Month 3	Month 4	Month 5	Month 6
Brand Tools and Template	▓					
Software – Instruction & Training		▓	▓	▓	▓	▓
Style Guide & Look Book	▓	▓				
Pitch Deck & Sales Sheet			▓	▓		
Web Site Page/Tab					▓	
Marketing & Awareness Took Kit						▓
Category Prioritization			▓			
Identify List of Prospect Licensees				▓		
Identify Other Activities					▓	

Case # 9 – Better Homes and Gardens Real Estate Signs 100-Year Deal

Meredith Corporation has a license with Anywhere Real Estate, Inc. (formerly known as Realogy Corporation) for Better Homes and Gardens Real Estate Services. Better Homes and Gardens Real Estate is a franchise company with approximately 400 independently owned and operated offices and 12,000 independent sales associates. The initial term began in October 2007 and is 50 years with a renewal provision for an additional 50-year term. Two well-known companies with a track record of outstanding performance have established a licensing agreement to sublicense the name for real estate brokerage services.

Licensor: Meredith Operations Corporation (formerly Meredith Corporation)
Licensee: Anywhere Real Estate, Inc. (formerly known as Realogy Corporation)
Licensed Property: Better Homes and Gardens
Category: Real Estate Services

FIGURE 4.7   Better Homes & Gardens Realty
Source: Credit: Better Homes & Gardens

Situation: In 1978, Meredith Corporation, one of the nation's leading media and marketing companies and publisher of *Better Homes and Gardens* magazine, launched the former Better Homes and Gardens Real Estate Service. The Better Homes and Gardens brand has 97 percent brand recognition. The name is synonymous with quality and serves to create trust. After operating for 20 years, Meredith sold the real estate business to GMAC Home Services Inc., under an agreement for them to use the Better Homes and Gardens name for ten years. In 2007, Meredith saw the opportunity to continue in the real estate business with the Better Homes and Gardens brand.

Task: Continue to offer Better Home and Gardens real estate services by licensing the brand in that category. Find a best-in-class licensee with an extended term.

Action: On October 8, 2007, Meredith Corporation entered into a long-term agreement to license the Better Homes and Gardens® brand to Anywhere Real Estate Inc. (formerly known as Realogy Corporation). Anywhere, owner of brands such as CENTURY 21®,

Coldwell Banker® and ERA®, is using the brand to build a new residential real estate franchise system based on the Better Homes and Gardens brand. The term of the deal is 50 years with a 50-year renewal for a total of 100 years (Taylor, 2007).

Results: Meredith receives ongoing royalty payments from Anywhere based on a percentage of sales from the Better Homes and Gardens Real Estate franchise system. In addition, Anywhere purchases advertising in Meredith titles to market *Meredith* magazine subscriptions through the Better Homes and Garden Real Estate franchise system. Meredith leveraged the relationship to create additional advertising partnerships with existing and new clients and will offer Realogy selected database services.

Noteworthy: "This is a tremendous opportunity to capitalize on the power of America's leading consumer magazine brand on behalf of the world's most successful real estate franchise company," said Meredith President and Chief Executive Officer Steve Lacy. "It fits extremely well with our strategic objective to further diversify our business by providing Meredith with significant sources of revenue beyond traditional advertising." "Better Homes and Gardens is a powerful brand and we are actively seeking more licensing opportunities that fit our strategic objective of leveraging Meredith's brands and our 85-million name database on behalf of market-leading companies such as Realogy," said Meredith Chief Development Officer John S. Zieser. "We continue to pursue brand extensions that will serve consumers and advertisers alike and extend the reach and vitality of our brands." Meredith brand licensing activities include more than 3,000 SKUs of branded products at 4,000 Walmart stores across the US and at walmart.com (Slusark, 2019).

References

Ahrens, F. (2003). Disney presents Mickey Mouse, again. *Washington Post*. www.washingtonpost.com/archive/business/2003/07/26/disney-presents-mickey-mouse-again/817d6daf-b1d7-4577-8932-87447bfd1d66/

Canalichio, P. (2018). *Expand, grow, thrive: 5 Proven steps to turn good brands into global brands through the LASSO method*. Emerald Publishing Limited.

Canalichio, P. (2019). *Breakthrough licensing: A disciplined path to profitable brand extensions*. BrandAlive.

Goldscheider, R., & Gordon, A. (2006). *Licensing best practices: Strategic, territorial and technology issues*. John Wiley & Sons.

Parr, R. (2007). *Royalty rates for licensing intellectual property*. John Wiley & Sons.

Raugust, K. (2004). *The licensing business handbook*. EPM Communications.

Santo, A. (2015). *Selling the silver bullet: The lone ranger and transmedia brand licensing*. University of Texas Press.

Slusark, A. (2019). Meredith brand licensing activities include more than 3,000 SKUs of branded products at 4,000 Walmart stores across the U.S. Meredith Corporation. https://dotdashmeredith.mediaroom.com/2019-10-22-Meredith-Corporation-Sells-Money-Brand-To-Ad-Practitioners-LLC

Stone, M. (2018). *The power of licensing: Harnessing brand equity*. American Bar Association.

Taylor, P. (2007). *Meredith to license better homes and gardens brand to Realogy for creation of residential real estate franchise system*. Meredith Corporation.

APPENDIX 4.1

Deal Term Summary Sheet

Date: ____/____/____

This deal term summary sets forth certain deal terms for a proposed license agreement between the parties. The parties agree that this summary is not a contract and is not binding on either party. List details after the semicolon for each area.

Proposed Licensee:

Licensee address:

Type of entity and state under which Licensee is formed (e.g., a Delaware corporation):

Scope of License

Trademarks (list all trademarks to be licensed):

Covered Products (list all categories to be authorized in the license):

Authorized Channels (list all channel types to be authorized in the license):

Territory (list all countries or regions within a country to be authorized in the license):

Term (list the years for the term of the license):

Initial Term:

Extended Term (only upon mutual agreement of the parties):

Insurance Requirements (list insurance requirements of prospective licensee):

Required limits may be satisfied by a combination of primary General Products, Umbrella, and/or Excess Liability insurance policies

Royalty and Payment Terms

Royalty Rate (list the royalty rate or rates to be used):

Advance (list any advance payment required):

The Advance payment may be offset against Royalties due during the first year of the period.

***

Guaranteed Minimum Periodic Royalty Payments (by country and by period):

Initial Term	Year	Amount

In the event the parties elect to extend the Term of the Agreement for the Extended Term, the Guaranteed Minimum Periodic Royalty Payments for the Extended Term are:

Year	Amount

Marketing and Sales

Schedule of Minimum New Product Introductions (list number of new product introductions required per year):

Sales Performance Requirements (list the amount of revenue per year):

Year	Amount

Shipping Date (list the date product must be shipped by):

The Shipping Date means the date by which the Licensee must first ship Licensed Products to the retailers for sale by the retailers.

Commercialization Date (list the date the product must be in market):

The Commercialization Date is the date by which Licensee must have placement of each Licensed Product in no less than two of the top five retailers or other entities in each of the Authorized Channels in each country of the Territory.

Submitted for approval (Licensee):   **Approved (Licensor):**

Signature: _____   Signature: _____

Name: _____   Name: _____

Title: _____   Title: _____

Company Name: _____   Company Name: _____

Address: _____   Address: _____

APPENDIX 4.2

Agreeing to the Deal Terms – Mock Negotiation

After the brand owner (licensor) and the manufacturer (licensee) have understood all the deal terms and have structured a negotiation strategy in their mind, it is time to put their knowledge to work. They now need to get together and negotiate each of the deal terms. Only when they agree on each of the deal terms will their relationship reach the next level of actually drafting and signing the contract.

The precursor to the actual contract is the Deal Terms Sheet, which contains the most important deal terms that the licensee and the licensor need to agree upon. These deal terms, including trademarks licensed, covered products, territories, channels, royalty rates and so on, are terms that both parties will encounter during the day-to-day servicing of the license. Please see Figure Appendix 4.2 for an example of the Deal Terms Sheet.

The negotiation of the key deal terms usually takes place face-to-face. While you can negotiate these terms over the phone or even via email, there is nothing like gauging the other party's body language and facial expressions during any negotiation. As we mentioned in the previous section, communication is an important piece of the negotiation's framework. If both parties have thought through their negotiation's strategy in advance – that is, evaluated their alternatives, defined their BATNA and their interests – an agreement on the Deal Terms Sheet can be achieved in as little as one day.

The mock negotiation below is between Ms. Zerrillo, VP of Licensing for the Storage Solutions Brand (the licensor) and Mr. Doe, the CEO of Excellent Cabinets Corp. (prospective licensee). Excellent Cabinets is interested in licensing the Storage Solutions brand in the Ready-to-Assemble Wooden Shelves and Cabinets category. Excellent Cabinets is a well-respected company and already holds licenses of other prestigious brands in the category, including Shelves!, Woodblocker, Self Shelf, Garage Essentials and Storage Essentials.

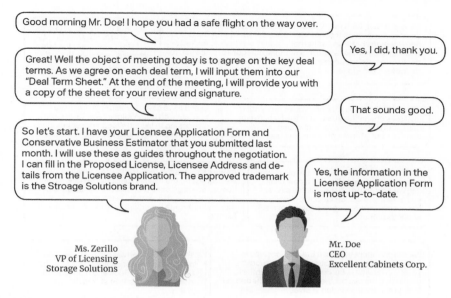

FIGURE APP 4.2.1   Mock Introduction

Deal Term Summary

March 10, 2025

This deal term summary set forth certain deal terms for a proposed license agreement between the parties. The parties agree that this summary is not a contract and is not binding on either party.

Proposed Licensee: Excellent Cabinets, Corp.
Licensee Address: 123 Cabinet Road, Little Rock, AR
Types of entity and state under which Licensee is found (e.g., a Delaware corporation):
An Arkansas Corporation

Scope of License

Trademarks: Storage Solutions
Covered Products: Ready-to-Assemble (RTA) Wood Garage Cabinets and Shelves
     including
     Oak Cabinets, Oak Shelves, Maple Cabinets Maple Shelves,
     Teak Cabinets, Teak Shelves
Authorized Channels: Mass (i.e., Walmart, Target), Home Improvement
     (i.e., Home Depot, Lowes), Department Stores
     (i.e., Kohls. JCPenney, Sears)
Territory: The US and Canada
Term: Initial Term: 4 Years
Extended Term: 3 Years

Okay, got that. Let's move to Covered Products. I see from your Licesee Application that you would like the license for the Storage Solutions brand in 6 differnet product categories. You're currently only commercialized in 5 of those categories. Since you're not selling any Oak Shelves, we can only grant you a license for the other 5 categories.

Yes, but we are expecting to launch Woodblocker branded Oak Cabinets in the Mass channel nationally this fall.

I didn't know that. Is that why you're requesting the Mass channel in addition to the Department Store and Home Improvement channels? You don't currently have a presence in Mass Channel.

Exactly! We have developed a great relationship with both Walmart and Target and are looking to launch Woodblocker branded Oak Shelves with these retailers in the fall.

OK. That addresses our fears of giving you a new product category and a new channel. We don't normally do this but since you're ready to launch Woodblocker in a few months, we feel comfortable. Let's talk about territories.

As we mentioned in the Licensee Application, we are requesting the license for all North America and Europe. We represent Woodblocker, Shelves, Self Shelf, and Garage Essentials in North America. We represent Storage Essentials in North America and Europe.

We are confident you have the relationships in North America to make our progress a success. What worries me is Europe. Storage Essentials dominates the plastic shelves market in Europe, but their presence in wooden shelves is negligible.

Yes, I supose you are right. We are planning to increase shelf space for Storage Essential's Teak, Rose and Maple wood shelves in the current stores that we sell in.

Well, keep us posted on how that goes. We may re-consider Europe for the extended terms. For the current term, we will stick with North America. Speaking of term, we normally sign 3-year contracts with a 3-year extended period.

We will need 18 months to get concept approved, attend line reviews with retailers, book orders, and ship product to the stores. That will give us another 18 months on the shelf at the end of the first term. We would like to get a full two years. How about we push the term to four years?

FIGURE APP 4.2.2 Mock Covered Products

Marketing and Sales

Schedule of Minimum New Product Introductions (per year): 3

Sales Performance Requirements (per year):

Year	Amount
YR 1	$800,000
YR 2	$1,654,545
YR 3	$2,757,575
YR 4	$3,171,212
YR 5	$3,446,969
YR 6	$3,860,606
YR 7	$4,687,878

FIGURE APP 4.2.3   Mock Sales Performance

Shipping Date: 6–9 Months after Contract Execution

The Shipping Date means the date by which the Licensee must first ship Licensed Products to the retailers for sale by retailers.

Commercialization Date: 1–3 Months after Shipping Date

The Commercialization Date is the date by which Licensee must have placement of each Licensed Product in no less than two of the top five retailers or other entities in each of the Authorized Channels in each country of the Territory.

So what I'm hearing you say is 18 months from today, you will be ready for commercialization. Today is March 10, 2019. You will be ready to commercialize on August 10, 2020?

Well, technically, yes, but it also depends on our line reviews with the retailers. We need at least 8 months after the line reviews to make and ship product.

That makes sense. We will work with you to ensure there are no delays from our end. When are the line reviews expected to take place?

The schedule for the next set of line reviews is awaited from the retailers. However, they usually take place in January every year.

So, if your line reviews were held in January 2020, you would technically be able to commercialize in August 2020. Let's just add a couple of months of buffer and assume the line reviews happen in March 2021. Then, you will be able to commercialize by October 10, 2021.

Yes, I appreciate the buffer. Thank you. October 10, 2020 seems reasonable. To be able to commercialize on October 10, I will ship by September 1, 2020.

FIGURE APP 4.2.4 Mock Commercialization Date

Sure. We want to set you up for a successful start! Moving on, our stand royalty rate is 10%.

Yes, I understand that it is the going rate for a brand of your stature. However, the margins on most of your licensed products are probably higher than 40%. RTA Wooden Shelves and Cabinets just don't afford these kinds of margins.

I see. What sort of royalty rate would you be comfortable with?

Well our margins are generally in the 25% - 30% range. Given this, we would be willing to pay a 7% royalty rate. We don't want to price ourselves out of the market!

Can you explain how you reached that number?

That's the going rate in the market for some of your direct competitors.

Well, based on your analysis, if you sold $800,000 worth of product at a 40% margin and paid us 10% in royalty, we would earn $80,000 and you would earn $148,571. Now you said your margin won't exceed 30%. At a 30% margin, if you paid us 7.25% as royalty, both of our earnings would fall by $21,978 each. We're willing to share the burder of the lower margins with you, but we will not aaccept a royalty rate lower than 7.25%.

I cannot argue with that! Yes, I think 7.25% is a fair rate.

I'm glad we agree. We also usually ask for 50% of the first year minimum guaranteed royalty payments as a cash advance upon signing the contract.

Okay. What are the minimum guaranteed royalty payments in this case?

Well, we agreed upon the minimum sales target to be $800,000 in the first year. So the minimum guaranteed royalty payments iwll have to be $58,022. Half of that amount, $29,011 will be the cash advance.

And this will be paid at the time of signing the contract?

That's correct. The cash advance will be offset against future royalty payments. We also require you to hold insurance with a minimum of $1 million coverage. We really don't have much bandwidth here.

I understand and will contact my insurance provider.

Well, Mr. Doe, it looks like we have agreed to all deal terms. I will send you a copy of the Deal Terms Sheet for you to review and sign.

Sure, thank you Ms. Z, I look forward to working with you in the future!

FIGURE APP 4.2.5 Mock Royalty Rate & Minimum

APPENDIX 4.3

Senior Executive Approval Memo Guidelines

In best-in-class organizations, the licensor's team has to gain approval from the CEO or the senior management of their company before they can actually sign the contract. This stage may be overlooked for smaller-sized deals. In the case of larger deals, where the expected royalty revenue exceeds $1 million, a memo outlining the details of the agreement is prepared by the licensing team and with the help of the business unit that is licensing their brand. The key questions addressed in the memo are:

A. Can the licensee deliver reliable quality and service levels?
B. How will it help the brand?
C. Does the financial return justify our time and total efforts?

The memo contains background information on the product category such as the size of the market, the players, success factors and consumer insight. It covers the history of the product category and the brand and makes a case for why the chosen product category is a good fit for the brand and the company. It addresses the rationale behind licensing the category as opposed to manufacturing or sourcing it and why it makes sense to invest in the project. Included with the memo is a summary of the licensing agreement, any pictures of current product made by the licensee, and physical samples, if available. Please see an example of a typical Memo to the CEO below.

The licensee must keep in mind that even though the licensee has signed the Deal Terms Sheet, the licensor can walk away from the agreement at any point. Typically, the licensor needs approval from their senior management before they can sign off on any deal.

Sample: Memo to the CEO

To:	[Name] CEO
From:	[Name] VP of Licensing
Cc:	Head of STORAGE SOLUTIONS Brand

Brand Manager of STORAGE SOLUTIONS Brand

Subject: Licensing Approval Request: Licensee, EXCELLENT CABINETS, for STORAGE SOLUTIONS Branded Ready-to-Assemble (RTA) wooden garage cabinets and shelves

Date: March 10, 2024

Sir,

We have a signed contract from Excellent Cabinets, Corp. to license RTA wooden garage cabinets and shelves under the STORAGE SOLUTIONS brand. This license will enable STORAGE SOLUTIONS to improve its current cabinets and shelves product line while maximizing profitability. Immediate execution of this contract is necessary to capture 2025 opportunities.

This memo requests your approval for me to sign this contract with Excellent Cabinets.

Background

US retail sales of wooden garage cabinets and shelves are estimated at $900 million (60% branded within the specialty and mass channels).

Category success is largely defined by (1) SKU management core competency; (2) a vendor's commitment to develop, redesign and replace SKUs rapidly throughout the year; and (3) funding and programming to influence product trial.

In the first quarter of 2019, STORAGE SOLUTIONS conducted an Internet survey of 500+ consumers to determine the brand's extendibility within the wooden garage cabinets and shelves category. This research indicated 90 percent of consumers believed STORAGE SOLUTIONS fit within the category, and STORAGE SOLUTIONS entered the category with retailer-specific styles for tests at Walmart, Target and The Home Depot in January 2021. Six months later, the program was deemed a failure by these retailers and was discontinued for 2022. STORAGE SOLUTIONS then decided to exit the category based on this lack of success and service issues with its two suppliers for the line.

In December of 2022, Walmart management reversed its decision and requested that STORAGE SOLUTIONS continue providing them with the line in 2017. STORAGE SOLUTIONS unsuccessfully attempted to influence Walmart to seek the products from another vendor by explaining STORAGE SOLUTIONS' ongoing supplier issues for the line and its inability to refresh any element of the product offering from 2022.

STORAGE SOLUTIONS' Category Sales (and Standard Margin)

Trade Sales	Year
$ 1.7 MM (45.6%)	2021
$ 2.1 MM (42.6%)	2022
$ 1.5 MM (39.8%)	2023

Program performance has continued to decline. STORAGE SOLUTIONS' sales of wooden garage cabinets and shelves to Walmart this year are estimated to drop 29 percent from $2.1 million in 2009 to $1.5 million in 2023. Close-out stores now account for 14 percent of the sales this year for a total sales estimate of $1.5 million in 2023. This is less than 3 percent of Walmart's total wooden garage cabinets and shelves business. Walmart and STORAGE SOLUTIONS have jointly agreed to close out this business in 2024 due to program service issues and STORAGE SOLUTIONS lack of attention to this segment.

STORAGE SOLUTIONS believes that the wooden garage cabinets and shelves category is a good fit for the STORAGE SOLUTIONS brand (more on this later). However, the STORAGE SOLUTIONS business system is not ideally configured to support the dynamics of the category and lacks the capabilities critical to its success:

A. The program is SKU intensive: good programs require offering retailers product lines in excess of 25 different products.
B. Order sizes, while moderate, are highly variable.
C. The program is a drain on resources, requiring a full-time product manager, engineer and sourcing specialist, along with substantial Channel Marketing time.
D. Division SG&A costs against the program are approximately $600,000–$800,000 annually.
E. Current ROI on the business is approximately $420,000 (20%).

The above factors combined with STORAGE SOLUTIONS; current investment priorities result in STORAGE SOLUTIONS' decision to remain in the category, but to do so via a licensing relationship with a well-positioned market leader.

The following four companies have 65 percent of the wooden garage cabinets and shelves category (approximately 35% is private label):

- Topshelf Brands with 20 percent market share.
- AAA Storage with 20 percent market share.
- Excellent Cabinets with 15 percent market share.
- PDQ Cabinets with 10 percent market share.

We approached Topshelf Brands and Excellent Cabinets based on their demonstrated success as a licensor of other major brands and the strength of their reputations in the category. Additionally, Global Licensing established a relationship with STORAGE SOLUTIONS in 2020, and they are currently a licensee for Shelves! for wooden garage cabinets and shelves under the Cabinet Essentials and Building Shelves sub-branded programs at Target and Lowe's only. Both Topshelf Brands and Excellent Cabinets expressed interest in a STORAGE SOLUTIONS license.

As referenced above, Topshelf Brands manages a broad line of Shelf Aid products including tools and gadgets, and ready-to-assemble shelves and cabinets; in addition to mass distribution, the Shelf Aid line also sells at Bed, Bath & Beyond and other specialty channels, directly competing with Shelves! core cabinets and shelves program.

With licenses including Shelves!, Self Shelf, Woodblocker, Garage Essentials and Storage Plus, Excellent Cabinets has a deep understanding of each brand's equities and their positioning within the retail landscape.

Excellent Cabinets believes the STORAGE SOLUTIONS brand should be positioned at the Mid Price Point/High Price Point level and can achieve success in the mass, club and specialty channels while also maintaining the unique positioning of its Shelves! line.

Rationale

Mr. CEO, you asked us to specifically address three questions when making these recommendations to you:

A. Can the licensee deliver reliable quality and service levels?

Yes, they can. In fact, Excellent Cabinets was selected as The Home Depot Vendor of the Year in 2020, 2021 and 2022 for cabinets and shelves.

Founded in 1921 as Excellent Cabinets, Corp., Excellent Cabinets evolved as a manufacturer of quality cabinets, shelves, fine tools and gadgets. Excellent Cabinets now markets more than 100 items to retailers and wholesalers based in North America and more than 100,000 pieces are shipped each week from its warehouse in Little Rock, AR. All products undergo extensive pre-introduction prototype testing, and all products are inspected at their source, whether made in the US, Europe or Asia.

Based on Excellent Cabinets' reliable quality, service levels and brand and product management capabilities, Excellent Cabinets has held the Garage Essentials license for 10 years, the Self Shelf license for 8 years and the Storage Plus license for 3 years. In 2019, in addition to the Shelves! license, Excellent Cabinets also acquired the Woodblocker license.

B. How will it help the brand?

1. Quality product: STORAGE SOLUTIONS will ensure Excellent Cabinets develops intelligently designed and stylish products, enhancing the consumers' overall level of satisfaction.
   This purposeful innovation will enable the consumer to feel more "relaxed and in control" when he is renovating his garage. Excellent Cabinets has a deep understanding of the wooden garage cabinets and shelves industry; they will have dedicated and skilled product managers, engineers, designers and sourcing specialists assigned full-time to the brand.
2. Availability: We will offer greater exposure for the brand – Excellent Cabinets has strong retail relationships with buyers in channels where STORAGE SOLUTIONS is not strong. This creates opportunities to place STORAGE SOLUTIONS wooden garage cabinets and shelves into retailers where we currently have no presence.
3. "Free up" resources to focus on brand: Focus will result in more ROI – Excellent Cabinets can execute a world-class wooden garage cabinets and shelves program with minimal input from our organization. Licensing to Excellent Cabinets frees up our own resources allowing STORAGE SOLUTIONS to execute alternate programs aligned with our internal competencies.

Supporting Data

1. 55% of consumers stated they were satisfied with the solutions offered by products designed to organize the garage. (6/20XX IPSOS Shifrin N = 3,322)

2. 50% of consumers said the wooden garage cabinets and shelves category "fits extremely well or fits very well" with our brand. (8/20XX Zoomerang Study N = approx 350)
3. For the wooden garage cabinets and shelves category, STORAGE SOLUTIONS had 97% aided awareness, Cabinet Aid 88%, AAA 17%. Consumers expect to see us in the category. (IPSOS, A&U, I&A Study 5/20XX)
4. Of the brands most recently purchased in wooden garage cabinets and shelves, 24% said STORAGE SOLUTIONS, 21% said Cabinet Aid and 10% said AAA. (IPSOS, A&U, I&A Study 5/20XX)
5. #1 reason consumers select a brand in the wooden garage cabinets and shelves category (92% top 2 box) is DURABILITY. This is our key brand equity. (IPSOS, A&U, I&A Study 5/20XX)

C. Does the financial return justify our time and total efforts with STORAGE SOLUTIONS?

Excellent Cabinets is well positioned to assume and grow the existing wooden garage cabinets and shelves program. While Excellent Cabinets' minimum royalty commitment for 2026 is $120,000, we expect earned royalty revenues to exceed $300,000 in the first year.

This contract is written for an initial term of four years so that Excellent Cabinets may fully invest in the STORAGE SOLUTIONS brand. As a result, we expect the royalties to exceed $500,000 by 2028 as Excellent Cabinets expands its sales beyond exceed $800,000. Mass to the specialty, department store and home center channels. Projections for years 2031 and beyond exceed $2 million.

APPENDIX 4.4

Licensor–Licensee Orientation Meeting

Agenda – [Date]

Licensee Attendees:

[Name] – Chief Marketing Officer
[Name] – VP Brand
[Name] – VP Digital
[Name] – VP or Director Product Development
[Name] – VP or Director Partnership
[Name] – Account/Licensing Manager

Licensor Attendees:

[Name] – VP Product Innovation/Research
[Name] – VP Brand/Digital
[Name] – VP Business Development
[Name] – VP Marketing Communications
[Name] – VP or Director Innovation
[Name] – VP or Director of Licensing
[Name] – Director of Operations

Topic	Time	Lead
Welcome Message	9:00am	[Senior Executive, Licensor]
Introductions	9:15am	All Members
Voice of the [Licensor] Brand	9:30am	VP Marketing Communications [Licensor]
Voice of [Licensee] Brand	9:45am	VP Brand [Licensee, if applicable]
Licensee Program Positioning Proposals and discussion	10:00am	Product Branding Examples by Channel VP Product Development [Licensee]
Marketing Calendar Review	11:00am	Licensor and Licensee Representatives to review calendar for collaboration
Lunch	12:00pm	All Members
Graphic & Design Overview – Licensor Brand Standards	12:30pm	VP Brand/Digital [Licensor]
Quality Assurance Overview – Licensor Product Standards	12:50pm	VP Product Innovation/Research [Licensor]
Approval Process Overview • Process • Process Forms • Pipeline Report Testing Standards	2:30pm	VP/Director of Licensing [Licensor]

Topic	Time	Lead
Financial Reports • Business Plan • Dashboard Royalty Reports	3:00pm	VP/Director of Licensing [Licensor]
Next Steps • Review Project Calendar • Next steps/meeting	3:30pm	All Members
Meeting Close	4:00pm	All Members

APPENDIX 4.5

Establishing a Business Plan

The business plan created is a critical component in ensuring the success of a brand licensing program. When the licensor works side-by-side with the licensee and monitors the success of the licensee's business with their brand in the marketplace, their success will be enhanced. This appendix covers how to understand the licensee's business plans and ensure alignment with the licensors business objectives to develop steps toward success.

Once the licensor has signed the contract and made sure the licensee has a good understanding of the brand, it is essential to give the licensee the right tools to be successful. Monitoring the licensee's business and ensuring that they set achievable targets empowers the licensee to maximize the license. From a business planning perspective, this entails Sales Management, Marketing Management, and Quality and Compliance Management. **Sales Management** business planning can be broken down into annual, quarterly, or monthly business plans. An Annual Business Plan traditionally gets developed in the third quarter of the prior year to the next year's business plan. While Sales Management business planning can be broken down into quarters, the **Marketing Management** planning is generally created as an Annual Business Plan. In this Annual Business Plan, the licensee should explain what they intend to do with the brand in that category, what they are going to spend to achieve their goals and how they will align the marketing mix with the licensor's brand marketing. Once discussed, they should then agree to the budget and how the budget will be spent. **Quality and Compliance Management** is neither broken down quarterly or annually; it's an ongoing planning that never ends. This critical piece makes sure that the quality of the products improves or is maintained through an ongoing program that's established by the licensee's quality team on a daily or weekly basis.

The Annual Business Plan, for the licensee, is also typically developed in the third quarter of the year prior to when the plan is being invoked. Once developed it will be reviewed by the key management team of the licensee and then shared with the licensor's team. The materials that are included in this plan are traditionally what are included in any business plan. The template provided shares the minimum requirements needed to ensure success. The key elements included in this Annual Business Plan are Sales Forecast, Royalty Forecast, Line Review Dates and other Key Retailer Dates. There are also "stretch" goals for each. The Sales and Royalty Forecasts are represented by region, channel and product. Line Review Dates focus on the dates that the licensee will meet with the retailer to discuss the products and sales. The Key Retailer Dates include major presentations, initiatives that are being done and innovative products that they should consider as part of their updated modular set in the ongoing sales of the licensed product in their stores. Below is a snapshot of the **Annual Business Plan** including standard and stretch goals.

Annual Business Plan

Licensee Name	Licensee #1	Year 2 Licensor Budget:	3,000,000
Submission Date:	Year 2	Year 2 Licensee Budget:	350,000
Royalty Rates (%):	5, 7.5, 10	Licensee Contribution:	12%
Minimum Guarantees:	100,000		
		Year 2 Licensor Estimate:	3,500,000
		Year 2 Licensee Estimate:	375,000
		Licensee Contribution:	11%

Sales & Royalty Summary Goal

	Year 1	Year 2		Comparison	
				Yr 1 Actual vs.	Yr 2 Budget vs.
	Actual	Budget	Estimate	Yr 2 Budget	Estimate
Sales	2,500,000	3,500,000	3,750,000	40%	7%
Royalites	250,000	350,000	375,000	40%	7%

Retailer Summary Goal

	Year 1		Year 2		
Retailer	Sales	Royalties	Sales	Royalties	% of Estimate
Walmart	658,000	65,800	770,000	77,000	21%
Target	475,000	47,500	573,000	57,300	15%
The Home Depot	378,000	37,800	425,000	42,500	11%
Lowe's	299,000	29,900	411,000	41,100	11%
SAM's Club	108,000	10,800	379,000	37,900	10%
Costco	107,000	10,700	368,000	36,800	10%
SEARS	97,000	9,700	320,000	32,000	9%
Kmart	75,000	7,500	144,000	14,400	4%
Kohl's	55,000	5,500	110,000	11,000	3%
Other	248,000	24,800	250,000	25,000	7%
Total	2,500,000	250,000	3,750,000	375,000	100%

Product Summary Goal

	Year 1		Year 2		
Product	Sales	Royalties	Sales	Royalties	% of Estimate
A	658,000	65,800	770,000	77,000	21%
B	475,000	47,500	573,000	57,300	15%
C	378,000	37,800	425,000	42,500	11%
D	299,000	29,900	411,000	41,100	11%
E	108,000	10,800	379,000	37,900	10%
F	107,000	10,700	368,000	36,800	10%
G	97,000	9,700	320,000	32,000	9%
H	75,000	7,500	144,000	14,400	4%
I	55,000	5,500	110,000	11,000	3%
J	248,000	24,800	250,000	25,000	7%
Total	2,500,000	250,000	3,750,000	375,000	100%

FIGURE APP 4.5.1 Annual Business Plan

Sales & Royalty Summary Stretch

	Year 1	Year 2		Comparison	
	Actual	Budget	Estimate	Yr 1 Actual vs. Yr 2 Budget	Yr 2 Budget vs. Estimate
Sales	2,500,000	3,500,000	3,750,000	40%	7%
Royalites	250,000	350,000	375,000	40%	7%

Retailer Summary Stretch

Retailer	Year 1		Year 2		
	Sales	Royalties	Sales	Royalties	% of Estimate
Walmart	658,000	65,800	1,000,000	77,000	21%
Target	475,000	47,500	700,000	57,300	15%
The Home Depot	378,000	37,800	450,000	42,500	11%
Lowe's	299,000	29,900	425,000	41,100	11%
SAM's Club	108,000	10,800	379,000	37,900	10%
Costco	107,000	10,700	368,000	36,800	10%
SEARS	97,000	9,700	320,000	32,000	9%
Kmart	75,000	7,500	144,000	14,400	4%
Kohl's	55,000	5,500	110,000	11,000	3%
Other	248,000	24,800	250,000	25,000	7%
Total	2,500,000	250,000	4,186,000	375,000	100%

Product Summary Stretch

Product	Year 1		Year 2		
	Sales	Royalties	Sales	Royalties	% of Estimate
A	658,000	65,800	900,000	77,000	21%
B	475,000	47,500	573,000	57,300	15%
C	378,000	37,800	425,000	42,500	11%
D	299,000	29,900	500,000	41,100	11%
E	108,000	10,800	379,000	37,900	10%
F	107,000	10,700	468,000	36,800	10%
G	97,000	9,700	320,000	32,000	9%
H	75,000	7,500	144,000	14,400	4%
I	55,000	5,500	227,000	11,000	3%
J	248,000	24,800	250,000	25,000	7%
Total	2,500,000	250,000	4,186,000	375,000	100%

FIGURE APP 4.5.2 Sales & Royalty Summary Stretch

As one can see, there is a lot involved with the business plan; each section is reviewed in detail below to better illustrate what exactly is expected from each party. Even though the licensor does not develop the Annual Business Plan, it is still vital that the licensor understands what it involves. The first section of the Annual Business Plan requests:

- The licensee's name
- The submission date
- The royalty rates
- The minimum guaranteed royalties for the year
- The licensor's budget
- The licensee's budget
- The licensee's contributions (budget)
- The licensor's estimate

- The licensee's estimate
- The licensee's contributions (estimate)

By taking a look at the estimates above, one can notice that the estimates relate to the budget. In this particular example, this plan was submitted in Year 2 of the contract; the royalty rates were 5 percent, 7.5 percent and 10 percent; and the Minimum Guarantee Royalty was a $100,000. The licensor's budget for the total business plan was $3 million; the licensee's budget was $350,000, which represented 12 percent of the overall licensor's budget. This percentage shows the significance of this program. The licensor's estimate for Year 2 is $3.5 million and the licensees estimate $375,000. In both these cases, they are estimated to exceed their budget amount for Year 1. The contribution is 11 percent, which is a bit lower percentage then the budgeted percentage of 12 percent.

When looking at the **Sales and Royalty Summary Goal** below, what one can see is the actual amounts in Year 1 were $2.5M for the licensor and $250,000 in royalties. For Year 2, there was $3.5M for the budget, and the royalties were $350,000. The estimate is $3.75M at a 10 percent royalty rate, which equals $375,000. In Year 2 the *actual* budget versus the *estimated* budget is compared and shows an increase by 40 percent. The *actual* budget versus the *estimate* budget also shows a difference of 7 percent. This is the kind of high-level detail the licensor would want in a business plan to know how they are faring compared to where they were in the previous year.

The **Retailer Summary Goal** by retailer is the next section to consider. In this particular case, all the retailers are listed on the left-hand side by the total number of sales projected. Starting with Walmart and ending with Kohl's one can see $658,000 in sales in Year 1 all the way down to $55,000 for Kohl's with Other at $248,000. The royalties correlated with that at 10 percent royalty rate is $250,000 on a base of $2.5M in sales. In Year 2, Walmart's amount is $770,000, and the total for the whole projection $3.75M.

Annual Business Plan

Licensee Name	Licensee #1	Year 2 Licensor Budget:	3,000,000
Submission Date:	Year 2	Year 2 Licensee Budget:	350,000
Royalty Rates (%):	5, 7.5, 10	Licensee Contribution:	12%
Minimum Guarantees:	100,000		
		Year 2 Licensor Estimate:	3,500,000
		Year 2 Licensee Estimate:	375,000
		Licensee Contribution:	11%

FIGURE APP 4.5.3 Annual Business Plan Header

Sales & Royalty Summary Goal

	Year 1	Year 2		Comparison	
				Yr 1 Actual vs.	Yr 2 Budget vs.
	Actual	Budget	Estimate	Yr 2 Budget	Estimate
Sales	2,500,000	3,500,000	3,750,000	40%	7%
Royalites	250,000	350,000	375,000	40%	7%

FIGURE APP 4.5.4 Sales & Royalty Summary Goal

The royalties generated are $375,000 in total, and the estimated percentage per retailer is outlined on the right-hand side, with Walmart at 21 percent all the way down to 3 percent for Kohl's; this totals to 100 percent for the royalties that are projected.

In the next section of the Annual Business Plan is the **Product Summary Goal.** For the sake of simplicity, the letters A–J identify the products. The sales are broken down in Year 1 similar to the retailer component and go from the largest to smallest in product percentages. Then Year 1 is compared to the Year 2 sales to provide a cross-reference between the retailers and the products in order for the licensor to see how the whole mix is completed and how it makes up 100 percent of the total sales that are going to be made.

Now it's time to look at the sales planning from a Quarterly Business Plan perspective. The Quarterly Business Plan discusses:

- Previous quarter meetings with the retailers and results
- Upcoming meetings
- Actual versus Estimates versus Budget for Sales and Royalties

  - How did the licensor do versus the estimate?
  - How did the licensor do versus the budget?

- Roadblocks to success
- Key elements to win

Retailer Summary Goal

Retailer	Year 1 Sales	Royalties	Year 2 Sales	Royalties	% of Estimate
Walmart	658,000	65,800	770,000	77,000	21%
Target	475,000	47,500	573,000	57,300	15%
The Home Depot	378,000	37,800	425,000	42,500	11%
Lowe's	299,000	29,900	411,000	41,100	11%
SAM's Club	108,000	10,800	379,000	37,900	10%
Costco	107,000	10,700	368,000	36,800	10%
SEARS	97,000	9,700	320,000	32,000	9%
Kmart	75,000	7,500	144,000	14,400	4%
Kohl's	55,000	5,500	110,000	11,000	3%
Other	248,000	24,800	250,000	25,000	7%
Total	2,500,000	250,000	3,750,000	375,000	100%

FIGURE APP 4.5.5   Retail Summary Goal

Product Summary Goal

Product	Year 1 Sales	Royalties	Year 2 Sales	Royalties	% of Estimate
A	658,000	65,800	770,000	77,000	21%
B	475,000	47,500	573,000	57,300	15%
C	378,000	37,800	425,000	42,500	11%
D	299,000	29,900	411,000	41,100	11%
E	108,000	10,800	379,000	37,900	10%
F	107,000	10,700	368,000	36,800	10%
G	97,000	9,700	320,000	32,000	9%
H	75,000	7,500	144,000	14,400	4%
I	55,000	5,500	110,000	11,000	3%
J	248,000	24,800	250,000	25,000	7%
Total	2,500,000	250,000	3,750,000	375,000	100%

FIGURE APP 4.5.6   Product Summary Goal

The budget component contains a bit more information and is reviewed below in detail. For example, if the budget is set in Month 9, what will be seen in the calendar year is an updated estimate that is provided every month. The *actuals* (Sales Recognized) are provided at the end of each month and can be revised to the budget numbers to include additional information that may impact the overall sales. This can include a new product that is going to market that is unanticipated which will either increase sales or shift their timing, thereby affecting one quarter versus the other. However, this excludes the overall business plan for the year from being affected. That's why when talking about *actual* versus *estimate* versus *budget*, the licensor does this for both the sales and royalties to see what impact it has on the overall program.

Roadblocks are another component that the licensee should address to ensure success. The licensee will want to establish a meeting with the DMM (District Marketing Manager) at each retailer as their support is critical to getting the next purchase order, especially if they are having trouble. It is not uncommon for the licensee to come to the licensor and say, "I am aware that you have a relationship with that DMM. Can you help us get them onboard so that we can ensure the success of our program?" Therefore, the licensor expects that there will be a multitude of roadblocks to address as they analyze the quarterly reviews. In addition to roadblocks, other key elements are discussed such as: What do those elements to win resemble? How important is one meeting versus another? Is this important product development? What are the specific approvals that are needed to meet a shipment date? This type of detail goes into a quarterly review book of the business plan.

In continuation, the **Monthly Business Plan** for sales planning includes:

- Sales calls
- Changes to forecasts
- Challenges

  - Sales
  - Approvals
  - Anything else that impacts the program's success

This is a more detailed program. Once can see that an Annual Business Plan is primarily strategic and a Quarterly Business Plan is strategic and tactical; the Monthly Business Plan tends to be tactical.

The **Monthly Licensee Dashboard**:

- Ties to Annual Business Plan
- Is updated monthly
- Provides key information: budget, forecast, sales/royalties by retailer and product, key dates

This Monthly Licensee Dashboard is an ongoing plan with updates on a monthly basis. In addition to that, there are weekly conversations that are less formal and help ensure the success of the overall program and that everybody is meeting individual goals.

Here is a snapshot of the Monthly Licensee Dashboard.

With an in-depth look into the Monthly Licensee Dashboard, one can see it is similar to the Annual Business Plan. The numbers at the top are exactly the same as far as who it is, when it's submitted, the targeted numbers and the percentages formulated. The subsection below, with respect to the sales and royalty summary, depicts the actual numbers and a comparison of the actual versus the estimate.

As it relates to the retailer section, the same thing is occurring on a monthly basis. The format is exactly the same, but now the licensee will be using *actuals* versus *estimates* on a monthly basis as it relates to sales, royalties and percentage of the estimate on a full-year basis. When looking at the left-hand side, at the actual numbers for that particular month, one can see that this is the same type of format used in the Annual Business Plan where there is a drilldown on a product basis with the exact relationship of the review versus the month actuals for the full year. This allows the licensor and the licensee to know if there is

Licensee Dashboard

Licensee Name	Licensee #1	Year 2 Licensor Budget:	3,000,000
Submission Date:	Year 2	Year 2 Licensee Budget:	350,000
Royalty Rates (%):	5, 7.5, 10	Licensee Contribution:	12%
Minimum Guarantees:	100,000		
		Year 2 Licensor Estimate:	3,500,000
		Year 2 Licensee Estimate:	375,000
		Licensee Contribution:	11%

Sales & Royalty Summary Goal

	Year 1	Year 2		Comparison	
				Yr 1 Actual vs.	Yr 2 Budget vs.
	Actual	Budget	Estimate	Yr 2 Budget	Estimate
Sales	2,500,000	3,500,000	3,750,000	40%	7%
Royalites	250,000	350,000	375,000	40%	7%

Retailer Summary Goal

	Year 1		Year 2		
Retailer	Sales	Royalties	Sales	Royalties	% of Estimate
Walmart	658,000	65,800	770,000	77,000	21%
Target	475,000	47,500	573,000	57,300	15%
The Home Depot	378,000	37,800	425,000	42,500	11%
Lowe's	299,000	29,900	411,000	41,100	11%
SAM's Club	108,000	10,800	379,000	37,900	10%
Costco	107,000	10,700	368,000	36,800	10%
SEARS	97,000	9,700	320,000	32,000	9%
Kmart	75,000	7,500	144,000	14,400	4%
Kohl's	55,000	5,500	110,000	11,000	3%
Other	248,000	24,800	250,000	25,000	7%
Total	2,500,000	250,000	3,750,000	375,000	100%

Product Summary Goal

	Year 1		Year 2		
Product	Sales	Royalties	Sales	Royalties	% of Estimate
A	658,000	65,800	770,000	77,000	21%
B	475,000	47,500	573,000	57,300	15%
C	378,000	37,800	425,000	42,500	11%
D	299,000	29,900	411,000	41,100	11%
E	108,000	10,800	379,000	37,900	10%
F	107,000	10,700	368,000	36,800	10%
G	97,000	9,700	320,000	32,000	9%
H	75,000	7,500	144,000	14,400	4%
I	55,000	5,500	110,000	11,000	3%
J	248,000	24,800	250,000	25,000	7%
Total	2,500,000	250,000	3,750,000	375,000	100%

FIGURE APP 4.5.7 Licensee Dashboard

a timing issue. Suppose there was a dip in one particular month, but the full year doesn't change. There may have been a small slip in the shipping date (by a couple of days), but it didn't have any impact on the overall success of the program.

Now that the licensor has a better understanding of the Sale Planning, they can shift their attention toward the Marketing Plan. Here the focus is to align the licensee with the licensor as it relates to key marketing initiatives for the coming year. Elements that are important to the licensor will include key changes in packaging, design, brand direction, fashions and anything that is an exclusive part of the program. At this point, the licensor brings all the licensees in to talk about their program from a holistic perspective. Areas that the licensor addresses include:

- Activities related to marketing
- Updates specific to the branding guidelines

From this "sit-down," the licensees take that information acquired and then build their business plan. Then they will illustrate what percentage of the total business they are going to allocate toward marketing. If it's 2 percent or 3 percent of the total sales of licensed product, it can range from $10,000 to $30,000. If this amount is multiplied by 10 or 20 licensees in the licensor's program, it can be a substantial increase to the overall marketing budget. This helps the licensor to compare these marketing budget numbers against their core business and see what the overall impact could be in strengthening the brand and helping to ensure the success of the program across all categories. Any key relationships are discussed here as well because it is important to know how the licensor and the licensee cooperate as it relates to advertising buys, PR initiatives and any other elements in the marketing mix to ensure the success of both the category and the overall brand on an annual basis.

The last piece of the business plan is **Quality and Compliance Management.** It is vital at this stage to review the contract compliance and what is taking place with the contract. The licensor wants to verify if the licensee is actually complying with all of the guidelines provided in the contract. That includes orientation, Annual Business Plan reviews and routine audits. Routine audits are important as the licensor moves forward with their licensing program. Sometimes issues are discovered that were not intentionally done incorrectly by the licensee such as a process oversight or information that has to be shared that would have helped the overall program improve and be more successful. Therefore, a routine audit should not be something the licensee should be concerned about if they are following the guidelines of the contract. The final are covered addresses Product Approvals and Financial Reporting. The licensor wants to know if those areas are being complied with as it relates to the contract. If yes, the success of the program is going to follow.

From the Quality Insurance perspective, the licensor is going to make routine site visits. These visits take place at the offices of the licensee or at their manufacturing facilities to make sure everything is in compliance, just as one would do so if that particular entity was part of their own company. This is not unusual and should include an examination of the supplier and manufacturer approvals to make sure that the products that are being provided by the suppliers and the manufacturers are meeting their own approval process without any gaps, slip-ups or problems. Finally, there is a QA report card that's taken to show where the licensee scores against a list of core criteria to assess the overall success of the quality of the program. This is foundationally important to ensure that products in the marketplace are meeting and exceeding standards.

5

BRAND LICENSING TIPS TO AVOID PITFALLS

Learning Objectives

The aim of the chapter is to provide tips and guides to answer the following questions: What are the kinds of expectations a licensor and a licensee could consider? What are the most frequent pitfalls experienced by licensors and licensees? How to avoid these pitfalls or to overcome them? What is the risk expectation? After reading this chapter, the reader will be able to critically analyze the strengths and weaknesses of a licensing program and suggest ways to avoid or overcome pitfalls and barriers to an enduring program.

Keywords: Pitfalls, Tips, Operational Risk, Strategic Risk, Expectations, Product Categories.

1. Pitfalls to Spot in the Brand Licensing Path

Licensing agreements could end with financial loss or damage to the brand's business, reputation or licensing program. Most likely this failure could have been caused by one or more brand licensing mistakes encountered in the brand licensing path. In this section, we look at the most frequent pitfalls to spot when operating under a licensing agreement and how to deal with them (Stone & Trebbien, 2019).

Pitfall 1: Overestimate Projections

This scenario happens when licensees desire a license from a brand owner so badly that they are willing to commit to any amount into their application and projections in order to acquire that license. In presence of information asymmetry, the brand owner doesn't know if the licensee is not able to actually achieve those results. With projections overstated, the licensor places the brand in a volatile situation if the projections offered are not delivered. In such circumstances there is a risk that the expected results will not be achieved, the Guaranteed Minimums Sales or Royalty commitments will not be met, and the program will collapse on itself. This overstated submission can harm the licensee's reputation by

DOI: 10.4324/9781003364566-6

placing him in the category of overpromising and underdelivering. The relationship with the brand owner could also be damaged. As a result, the brand owner likely will not renew the license with the licensee again, even though he was rated among the most qualified and suitable prospects. To avoid this pitfall, all parties involved should be realistic about the projections, size and scale of the licensing program even if it may involve the risk of not getting into the program.

Pitfall 2: Requesting Categories, Channels or Territories with no Capability to Execute

While this may seem the same as "Pitfall 1," it isn't. In this case, the licensee informs the brand owner of the channels, regions or categories to secure in the agreement. Instead of limiting the selection to the channels (or territories or categories) that provide the most financial success and benefit, the licensee gets the licensor to grant the rights to channels (or territories or categories) that make sense to the brand owner, even though the licensee is unable to commercialize. With this choice, there is the risk of leaving the most profitable channels (or territories or categories) barren of licensed products. To avoid this risk, it would be better to start out in a channel (or territory or category) that offers the highest chance for growth for the brand and then ask the brand owner for more channels, regions, categories once the parameters in the agreement are achieved.

Pitfall 3: Having Unrealistic Expectations

Unrealistic expectations happen when the partners do not understand the real strength of the brand licensed. Without an ample understanding of the strength of the brand, or its success, position and growth potential, the licensee could set goals for himself that are unachievable. Having realistic track record expectations propels the brand forward creating the conditions to meet revenue goals.

Pitfall 4: Applying the Licensed Trademark (Logo) on any Products

When a licensee acquires a brand and affixes the brand's logo onto any newly developed product (known as logo slapping) and does not take the time to build the brand's attributes into the product the program suffers. Putting a famous logo on any product does not always turn into high sales and profits for the licensee, and strong royalties for the licensor. However, this is not at all true. Consumers decipher when a newly developed product doesn't work with the brand. Instead of logo slapping, the licensee can custom design the brand's attributes into the product, while adhering to the brand's style guidelines. Playing to the brand's strengths is a way to expand the brand consistent with its value and attributes. Sesame Street helps kids grow stronger and kinder. One-third of the revenue comes from extending the Sesame Street brand through licensing. One way is by licensing their characters into the food category. They try to make a distinction between every day and "sometimes foods" more suitable for occasions like birthdays and celebrations. One of the brand strengths is that they have multiple characters. Their licensee, who creates fruit and vegetable purees for toddlers, is able to use a different character for each flavor. In the Netherlands, the company launched an anniversary campaign with our co-production partner. They commissioned an artist to do a rendition of Van Gogh painting,

"The Bedroom," where the artist painted the Sesame Street Muppet characters into the painting. The painting then drew kids into the Van Gogh Museum to see the painting while producing tremendous publicity for Sesame as well.

Pitfall 5: Failure to Follow the Approval Process

The approval process set by the brand owner is in place for many reasons. Failing to understand and follow the approval process fully according to the specifications given in the contract could result in the products not being approved. The potential of not hitting licensee revenue targets can put pressure on the manufacturer to sell unapproved licensed products. Selling unapproved products can be very risky and costly. For instance, consumers could file lawsuits against the licensee and the licensor, if the unapproved products were never tested and cause harm or fail to meet a government standard. A common mistake is expecting approvals to come easily and quickly. The approval process includes a number of steps that must be completed before a product is able to be consumed. If the licensee tries to get a program into a retailer without allowing the necessary amount of time to pass each phase of the approval process, the program will not be a success. This is why understanding the approval process helps licensees to avoid improper planning that can result in missing modular shipping and selling dates.

Pitfall 6: Not Knowing the Contract

Many different components are included in a contract such as deal terms, the approval process, the location in which the product will be sold, the royalty rate to be paid, the trademark to be used and much more. Being unfamiliar with the contract can strain the licensing relationship and ultimately result in termination of the contract. To avoid this pitfall, ensure that, once the licensing agreement is signed, everyone directly or indirectly involved in the brand licensing program is informed of the terms in the contract. This includes members of the sales, marketing, product development and design teams. To avoid this pitfall, a way is to purchase or license a licensing software. For instance, Brand-Comply by Octane5 is a software that incorporates each of the contract requirements into its platform, without needing to track them independently. Another way is to hire a specialized company, which uses a highly skilled group of employees to manage all the "back office" requirements of a licensing contract.

Pitfall 7: Not Prepared to Invest into the License

To reach the point where the license is acquired, the orientation is completed, and the business plan is finalized, both parties have invested a substantial amount of time (6–18 months) preparing for a license. Both partners have high expectations. If either one or both parties have not allocated enough resources for the execution of the license, there is a high likelihood the program will fail. Avoiding this pitfall requires the licensee and licensor to establish accountability within their respective organizations and match each party's level of investment. The licensor expects the licensee to plan to invest in the newly acquired brand in proportion to the agreement. The licensor also expects sales and brand growth along with the pursuit of every channel and every category designated by the contract. The licensee expects the licensor to market the brand, to provide support during sales calls and return quick approvals.

Pitfall 8: Trusting That the Licensor Has Your Best Interest at Heart

Sometimes licensors have their own agenda that may not be aligned with the licensee's agenda. Beware! A licensor may license a category they are vacating because they have strained a relationship with a retailer or failed in a category. Licensors may also choose to compete directly with the licensee or pitch one licensee against another. To avoid this pitfall, the parties should not assume that just because the contract was signed that the licensee and the licensor are entirely aligned. They should ensure all parties share the same vision and values.

Pitfall 9: Breaking the Rules or not Following the Written Contract

Everything that the licensee and the brand owner agreed upon is drawn up into a written contract which explicitly states the requirements of the licensing program. It may happen that the contract leaves some room for interpretation. Not following the written contract can put the parties in a dangerous situation or have a devastating financial impact on the business depending on the loss of revenue or the amount of the penalties the licensor requires the licensee to pay.

As an example, licensees who make the mistake of selling in unauthorized channels or territories, risk running into another licensee who has the rights to that specific channel (or territory) and has been selling in the same channel (or territory). This can create a significant amount of confusion in the marketplace, as well as incurring severe penalties incorporated in the contracts, up to and including termination. Ways to avoid this pitfall are to, first, have full knowledge of the contract's terms, conditions and boundaries and, second, not be tempted to sell licensed products outside the authorized channels or territory in order to meet the contractual Sales Minimums or Guaranteed Royalty commitments. To avoid any misunderstanding, the parties can ensure that a verbal request is followed by a confirmation email before proceeding.

Pitfall 10: Be Careful with a Company that Is New to Licensing from a Licensor Perspective

The licensor can be so excited about a new license to gloss over the licensee's lack of experience and understanding of what they are getting themselves into. Some companies think the license is enough to achieve their revenue goals. They don't think they need to market or promote the product, which is critical. Lack of a good forecasting that is integrated into a business plan can cause product development to take more than a year. The licensee can lose time getting to market and develop too many SKUs and run the risk of not earning the minimum guarantee. To avoid this pitfall, the licensee should carefully evaluate the licensor's experience and ensure the terms of the agreement support their expectations.

2.   Risk-Taking and Risk-Mitigation in Brand Licensing

Growth options come with risks such as growth risk, product development risk, market risk and operational risk (Mottner & Johnson, 2000). While business diversification can be a viable option to reduce risk, the benefits are mitigated by the need to grow faster and more profitably into new categories, channels or markets. A larger core business makes the brand diversification harder, because a new business should grow at many multiples of the existing business to contribute enough margins to reduce concentration risk. One way to limit the risk that comes with diversification is through brand licensing. In general, the risks associated with operating a brand licensing program are broad and if not managed can have an adverse impact on a brand. The licensee takes on the operational risk while the brand risk stays with the licensor. These two categories of risks associated with a brand licensing program are examined below.

Entering a new market via licensing has *lower product development risk* than extending the brand in house. In fact, there are several risk-limiting benefits to licensing a brand to a manufacturer of a product in the same category. To begin with, licensees possess resources and capabilities to manufacture the product and to market it, having done so for unbranded items or lesser-known brands. They have relationships with distributors and retailers that increase the opportunity to reach target market segments. In contrast, the licensor forgoes some control over distribution when choosing a licensing option. This lack of control can become a market risk when the licensee's positioning is not aligned with that of the licensor.

In addition, the whole point of a brand expansion strategy is speculating on what the market will require and seeing how it will integrate into the brand portfolio (Bass, 2004). But this can be risky. When Disney bought Marvel, many people thought they had paid too much for the comic brand, but Disney recognized that, for their business model, the opportunity to apply the Marvel portfolio to how they structure their entertainment would work well.

Once a company chooses to license its brand, it has two options on how to execute the program. If the licensor chooses to manage its program in house, a typical licensing program requires a team of individuals working together to ensure the program is managed properly. To reduce the management risk a company can choose a licensing agent, which includes some benefits such as:

- Less upfront investment. This means fewer internal full-time equivalent positions, variable versus fixed costs, which are driven by the revenue generated and a success-based commission structure.
- Easier and faster ramp-up. An agency can provide a turnkey solution and get products to market in 6 to 12 months versus 24 to 36 months if executed internally. Finally, it allows the company to maintain focus on their core business.
- Proof of concept established. This mitigates product adoption risk and helps to validate brand preference.

Brand licensing programs growth could come through additional licensees, greater numbers of approved licensed products, higher sales of licensed products, increased royalty rates or a combination of the above. On the surface a program growing year-over-year would seem to be run effectively. Often, however, these programs are not optimized and could even be at risk if a retailer chooses to drop a particular SKU or licensee. This is the case when a few of the SKUs, or the licensees, in the licensor portfolio account for most of the royalty revenue. The old 80/20 rule applies, where 20 percent of the SKUs, or the licensees (or both) bring in 80 percent of the revenue.

Brand expansion, which is also known as category extension, executed via licensing could be perceived as even more risky than brand extension (line extension). Here, brands broaden their presence into markets where they have not built their reputation, and, often, they rely on licensees to fill the experience and capacity gap on their behalf. Licensees take this risk for a range of reasons. The most powerful is that, where brand extension looks to achieve product continuation, brand expansion is based on emotional continuation. The brands are, in effect, intending to carry the emotional relationship which they have built with consumers from one sector to another (Wiedmann & Ludewig, 2008). It's a lateral jump, intended to achieve a greater "share of life." If the licensor hasn't selected the right category or the licensee is not equipped to tell the story through their licensed products, the program could suffer.

Licensees that operate with a smaller range of products, particularly those that wish to resource and oversee how they take those brands to market, generally choose to keep their assets close. With that comes a dependence on internal resources. There is the risk that the licensee, in this case, has underestimated others or overestimated its own abilities to expand into the current market, or another opportunity, using its own resources. When this happens, the licensee fails to take full advantage of its contractual rights limiting the effectiveness of the license.

Brands that prefer to take a more open approach in terms of having a larger product set and marketing them on a larger scale are also more likely to bring in licensing partnerships. The critical decisions that expose such companies to risk situations are twofold: finding who to partner with and finding ways to involve and include those partners in profitable and expandable ventures that do not jeopardize or compromise their core IP.

Sometimes, the structure of the licensee's business is completely disconnected from the licensing agreement (Meschnig et al., 2023). Brands under pressure to succeed strike deals with "any" licensing partner that shows up. Brand relevance is preferred over brand clarity, consistency and promise. When this happens, the execution is ineffective at best and disconnected at worst. Licensees don't know enough about the brand, don't have enough resources to execute the terms of the agreement or underestimate restrictions other than territory and channels. This puts brands at risk, especially when the licensors don't manage their programs well. This can result in licensed products that do not reflect the brand's attributes, a drop in servicing standards and out-of-stock instances.

One of the biggest challenges for licensors is fully executing licensing programs associated with their events. While the licensor has a strong desire to have licensed products sold at the events for the brand relevance, consumer connection and royalty revenue generated, few retail companies in general are willing to take the risk of buying event-specific merchandise. While the payoff can be huge, the program is fraught with risks, including obtaining sales permits, staffing for the event, gaining merchandise approvals, selecting the right mix of merchandise and, finally, finding the ideal locations where the crowds are expected to maximize the sale of merchandise.

Similar to the challenges that events present, licensors are enticed by partnering with celebrities due to their consumer appeal. People are drawn to iconic celebrities partly because of the memories they have of them but also because they often represent a lifestyle or dream that is exciting or inspiring. A licensing relationship with a celebrity gives brands incredible scale. Consider the benefits to brands like Keds, CoverGirl or even Apple, a partnership with Tailor Swift can bring. Of course, partnering with a celebrity has its risks. Tiger Woods' cheating scandal while married to Elin Nordegren that occurred in 2009, Michael Jackson dangling a small baby from a balcony in 2010, or Olympic swimmer

Ryan Lochte vandalizing a convenience store in Rio De Janeiro during the 2016 Summer Games brought significant negative exposure to their brand endorsers. Episodes like these can hurt the brand for a significant period of time as consumers judge these brands based on the behavior of the celebrity.

Companies that do not take control of their licensing programs are also likely to be less vigilant about things like counterfeiting because they are operating in a vacuum that separates them from their customers and keeps them at arm's length from their supply chains. When Mike Dunn founded Octane5, he did so because he saw that many companies with licensing programs were failing to resource compliance around their properties. Licensors weren't taking enough control of their assets, they had no analytics, their supply lines were opaque, and the brand was being executed in sloppy ways that led to misuse and misrepresentation. Failure to take ownership at this level quickly led to deeper risks.

In sum, the flip side of the mitigation risk due to growth, product development, market and operations for licensors is an increase in brand risk. The risk-taking that comes from brand licensing affects both licensors and licensees in a similar fashion. Each example reveals an increase in business risk, that is, poor business results that come from poor program management, brand expansion into a weak brand/wrong category, lack of licensee capability, selection of the wrong licensee, complexity of events, behavior of celebrities, theft from piracy/counterfeiting. These increases in business risk due to their nature almost always result in an increase in brand risk (Gibson, 2006).

EA SPORTS – FIFA PARTNERSHIP ENDS AFTER THREE DECADES

Consider the video game manufacturer who has developed an amazing soccer game. When they can acquire a license with the FIFA World Cup, they gain immediate access to the world's most popular sport.

For FIFA, the video game manufacturer and licensee is EA Sports, a division of Electronic Arts. According to the video game manufacturer, FIFA has always been the highlight of the year for the company in terms of sales; the licensing partnership between the two has run for almost three decades with branded game generating more than $20 billion in sales over the past two decades. With technological advancements, improved graphics, detailed visuals and new digital content features, the demand for FIFA increased exponentially from 2010 to 2013 with the number of FIFA units almost doubling from 6.4 million to 12.45 million. Only the best companies can obtain the rights to a license as big as the FIFA brand. However, this license will end at the FIFA Women's World Cup Championships in Australia/New Zealand in 2023. In addition to a doubling of EA Sports licensing fee, FIFA also demanded the ability to attach its brand to other digital products, including other video games. That proved to be a step too far for EA Sports, which now must persuade legions of devoted fans to get used to another name. According to Gareth Sutcliffe, a senior analyst specializing in the video games sector at Enders Analysis. "EA will continue to motor on: They have got all the technological smarts, the creative implementation of a fantastic football game – and it really is fantastic. But what do FIFA have? Their name. And then what?" To put the acquisition of a FIFA license in perspective, it is important to understand the global appeal of the FIFA brand and what FIFA expects from those charged to manage its IP (Panja, 2022).

Case # 10 – Michael Jordan's License with Nike Worth Billions

Jordan's deal with Nike will celebrate 40 years in 2024. The movie, Air, which hit theaters in 2023 reveals how the deal came together, the shoe companies involved and the advice of a wise mother that made it happen (Davids, 2023).

Licensor: Michael Jordan
Licensee: Nike, Inc.
Licensed Property: Michael Jordan's Name, Identity and Likeness

FIGURE 5.1   Nike Air Jordan Shoe
Source: Credit: iStock

In 1984, when Michael Jordan was about to get drafted into the NBA, he had three major sneaker brands (Adidas, Converse and Nike) vying for his signature. This gave Jordan significant leverage in negotiating terms and earning a contract that would suit his worth as an athlete. After hearing Nike's pitch, Jordan later would reveal how he asked Adidas if they could match it, out of nothing but loyalty. Adidas, worth $1.28 billion at the time, had been Jordan's first choice to sign. However, neither Adidas nor Converse were willing to match Nike's risk-taking offer. It was compelling for two reasons: no company had ever put forward terms in an athlete contract as lucrative as Nike and neither competitor needed Jordan as much as Nike with their plates filled with a line of star NBA players. On top of that Adidas was undergoing leadership changes, leading to dysfunctional behavior that unnerved Jordan.

Situation: Michael Jordan, the greatest basketball player of all time, and the third player in the NBA draft began his professional career in 1984 after winning a national championship in collegiate basketball at the University of North Carolina. At the time, he had signed a deal with Converse for one of their off-the-shelf shoes. When Adidas came courting in 1985, Nike (known for its running shoes) stepped into the picture. However, Jordan's agent,

David Falk, concerned with risk-mitigation with his star athlete, had no interest in Nike. Adidas was an established basketball brand with a line of top NBA talent.

Task: For Nike: sign Michael Jordan and revolutionize the perception of the company as a basketball shoe powerhouse. For Jordan: find a company that would pay royalties for his Name, Identity and Likeness (NIL), create a customized shoe that evoked the Jordan brand and position him as their preeminent NBA player.

Action: Nike executive Sonny Vaccaro convinced the owner, Phil Knight, to invest in Jordan, an unproven NBA player, and create a customized line of shoes known as the Air Jordan. Instead of a fee-only based arrangement, Jordan's mother negotiated a licensing agreement with Nike that formed the foundation of his trailblazing fortune. For both parties: establish a relationship that could hold up under the pressures of the NBA, Jordan's unrelenting competitiveness and the insatiable demands of the public. In spite of Jordan's retirement from the NBA in 2003, and the complexities of his personality that led him to try a career with Major League Baseball at the height of his NBA success in 1994 (Rawcliffe, 2022), the relationship has continued to thrive.

Results: Jordan's wealth, estimated in 2023 at $3.5 billion, stems from his Jordan brand apparel line at Nike, which was the subject of the Ben Affleck-directed film Air. Jordan's mother, Deloris, was integral in securing that deal (Albright & Pendleton, 2023). In 1984, Jordan signed a five-year contract with Nike for $2.5 million. The first pair of Air Jordans, the Air Jordan 1, was released in 1985 and became an instant hit. The popularity of the shoes, combined with Jordan's rising stardom and on-court success, propelled the Air Jordan brand to unparalleled heights. The partnership between Michael Jordan and Nike revolutionized athlete endorsements and branding in the sports industry, setting a precedent for lucrative and long-lasting collaborations. In 2022, the Jordan brand recorded $5.1 billion in revenue, representing almost 11 percent of Nike's total sales. The Bloomberg index calculation estimates Jordan earned a 5 percent royalty on Air Jordan's sales.

Noteworthy: Jordan's initial deal was a groundbreaking partnership offering him royalties on all sales of Jordan branded products and led to the creation of the iconic Air Jordan brand. At the time, Nike was looking to expand its presence in the basketball market, and they saw potential in signing Michael Jordan, who had just entered the NBA. What set this deal apart was the inclusion of a unique clause: the "royalty clause." This clause granted Jordan a percentage of the sales for every pair of Air Jordans that were sold. This was a departure from the usual endorsement deals of that time and proved to be a game-changer for both Nike and Jordan. And while there were other NBA players such as Chuck Taylor in 1917 and Clyde Drexler in 1973, who had had their own shoe, Nike took the Air Jordan line to new heights (Bowers, 2013). Since then, the Air Jordan line has become one of the most successful and recognizable sneaker brands globally, and Jordan's royalty deal with Nike is often cited as a prime example of how strategic partnerships can reshape industries (Baum, 2023). Today the Air Jordan brand has transcended basketball with many collegiate and professional athletes in soccer, American football and other sports wearing the brand (Stonebrook, 2022). Simeon Siegel, an analyst for BMO Capital Markets, said the Jordan brand has "transcended" him as a player. Many of (Nike's) customers are too young to have ever seen him play professional basketball. "Jordan the person and Jordan the brand have helped shape Nike as well as the entire athletic apparel landscape," reflected Siegel (Albright & Pendleton, 2023).

Jordan ended up signing with Nike and creating history with the brand. The $2.5-million deal has made Jordan the face of Nike and its basketball presence globally. Besides, Jordan's deal was a crucial business move for the Oregon-based company toward becoming a global sporting brand.

Air Jordan first started out being Jordan's line of shoes. However, in 1997, Nike formed a separate brand out of Jordan, with Jordan earning a 5 percent royalty from the profits. From 2017 to 2022, the Jordan brand earned $19.6 billion, which has benefited Nike massively.

References

Albright, A., & Pendleton, D. (2023). *Michael Jordan is the richest basketball player ever with $3.5 billion fortune*. Bloomberg.

Bass, A. (2004). Licensed extensions – stretching to communicate. *Journal of Brand Management*, *12*(1), 31–38.

Baum, B. (2023). *How Michael Jordan revolutionized the sneaker industry – and our relationship to shoes*. Temple University.

Bowers, B. (2013). *From Chuck Taylor to LeBron X: Year-by-year evolution of NBA sneakers. Bleacher report*. Turner Broadcasting.

Davids, B. (2023). Air' writer Alex Convery on the original plan for Michael Jordan and building Matt Damon's show-stopping monologue. *Hollywood Reporter*. www.hollywoodreporter.com/movies/movie-features/air-michael-jordan-was-shown-original-script-1235371417/

Gibson, J. (2006). Risk aversion and rights accretion in intellectual property law. *Yale Law Journal*, *116*, 882.

Meschnig, A., Decker-Lange, C., & Dubiel, A. (2023). Burning the candle at both ends: How to balance potential profitability and brand protection when licensing brands. *European Journal of Marketing*. https://kclpure.kcl.ac.uk/portal/en/publications/burning-the-candle-at-both-ends-how-to-balance-potential-profitab

Mottner, S., & Johnson, J. P. (2000). Motivations and risks in international licensing: A review and implications for licensing to transitional and emerging economies. *Journal of World Business*, *35*(2), 171–188.

Panja, T. (2022). *FIFA and EA sports end decades-long video game partnership*. New York Times.

Rawcliffe, T. (2022). Which team did Michael Jordan play baseball for? All you need to know. *Sportskeeda*. www.sportskeeda.com/basketball/which-team-michael-jordan-play-baseball-for-here-details

Stone, M., & Trebbien, J. D. (2019). Brand licensing: A powerful marketing tool for today's shopping battlefield. *Journal of Brand Strategy*, *8*(3), 207–217.

Stonebrook, I. (2022). Jordan Brand's big bet on football. *Boardroom*. https://boardroom.tv/jordan-brand-football-cleats-endorsements/

Wiedmann, K. P., & Ludewig, D. (2008). How risky are brand licensing strategies in view of customer perceptions and reactions? *Journal of General Management*, *33*(3), 31–52.

REMARKS

The Future of Licensing

Liz Kalodner

It is a privilege to read such a comprehensive textbook on the complicated, remarkable, sometimes enigmatic world of licensing. There was a time not so long ago where there was no roadmap, no GPS to guide us – when it was just intuition and salesmanship and sheer guts that drove the business. Those qualities are still critical to success in licensing, but there's more, and Pete Canalichio and Cristina Longo have created a manual to expose the many elements and aspects of licensing and led readers down a path of strategic planning, smooth, if not flawless, execution and productive partnership.

There are nuances of brands that cannot be taught, unknowable complications of an ever-changing retail environment, unforeseen scheduling changes and sometimes even irrational business stakeholders, but if you have mastered the fundamentals and understand the cautionary road signs, you will be well prepared to tackle those issues and succeed in this tremendously fun enterprise.

Licensing can certainly be a career unto itself, but it can also serve as a valuable part of any marketing mix – an additional way to connect with a fan, a viewer or a consumer. It does not need necessarily to encompass a multitude of categories. Sometimes one or two key products can make all the statements you need or want. And, if you're prepared, one or two key partnerships can last for a lifetime: Think Flintstones Vitamins, a partnership of 50 years, or Bubba Gump Shrimp Co. restaurants, now more than 25 years old. The authors have shown how to marry an understanding of a brand with the right kind of partner who can invest in a long-term strategy.

This book shows the complexity of a Business to Business industry that is ultimately about the relationship between a brand and the consumer. We are often taking an entity from a public medium and reaching into the home with a product that lives on a shelf, in a drawer or in a toy box to make a personal connection that can be affecting and long-lasting. Different brands enter licensing for different reasons, one no less valid than the other. Some want to extend the reach and exposure of the brand, some want to target a new audience, and sometimes, a brand sees an opportunity for a new, lucrative revenue stream. It's important to understand the value of the brand and its goals. And the timing needs to be right.

I was particularly taken by the section in this book on "Avoiding Pitfalls" as I remember too well making so many of those mistakes through the years. The R-rated action movies licensed to toys for kids who had never seen the film. The situation comedy licensed for a practical home kit which the audience couldn't take seriously. The model-oriented brand at a mass retailer not known for its fashion sense. We used to say all too often: "It seemed like a good idea at the time." With this book, that phrase might be eradicated. The chance to save time, money and angst is invaluable.

Licensing is a compelling field as it incorporates so many disciplines – legal in the negotiation and enforcement of contracts, creativity in graphic and industrial design, manufacturing and construction of different products and experiences, trade and consumer marketing to different audience segments, and retail strategy, sales, placement and analysis. Ultimately, licensing is a wonderful mix of innovation and business. It also presents constantly a chance to learn; as soon as you have sorted it out, there is a new product category, a new retailer, a new kind of partnership to study, to leverage, to master.

As you incorporate the lessons from this book, I encourage you to talk to your colleagues and competitors. They can also teach you, inspire you and partner with you. Licensing is collaborative and evolving, two qualities that make it a rewarding and fulfilling experience. I look forward to reading and seeing what you will accomplish in the years ahead.

Elizabeth Kalodner Biography

Most recently Executive Vice President and General Manager for CBS Consumer Products, Elizabeth Kalodner spent 10 years managing the multi-faceted, long-lived and much-loved Star Trek franchise as well as a vast portfolio of current TV franchises such as CSI and an extensive classic library of more than 150 titles, including The Twilight Zone and Cheers. Before coming to CBS, she was Executive Vice President and General Manager, Global Consumer Products for Sesame Workshop, handling the company's global-retail business including theme parks, touring shows, video/audio, toys, gifts, apparel and home furnishings. Prior to that, Liz Kalodner was Chairman and Chief Executive Officer of SocialNet, an Internet start-up and early entrant in the social networking space. She spent 10 years at The Walt Disney Company, where she worked in Film & Television Licensing and ran Walt Disney Records. She started her career in marketing at Kenner Products for classic brands like Play-Doh and Easy-Bake Oven. Liz Kalodner holds an undergraduate degree from Harvard University and an MBA, Marketing and Finance, from Columbia University.

INDEX

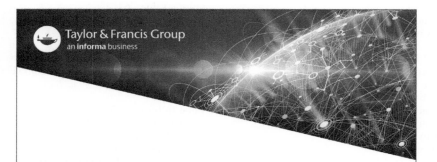

For Product Safety Concerns and Information please contact our
EU representative GPSR@taylorandfrancis.com Taylor & Francis
Verlag GmbH, Kaufingerstraße 24, 80331 München, Germany